Psychotypes

Salim Yolchiyev

Psychotypes

Copyright © 2022 by Salim Yolchiyev.

All rights reserved. No part of this book may be used or reproduced in any manner whatsoever without written permission except in the case of brief quotations embodied in critical articles or reviews.

ISBN: 9798404545791

Email: salim.yolchiyev1999@gmail.com

This book is dedicated to the best psychologist in the world:
my beloved mother, Madina Yolchiyeva

CONTENTS

WHAT IS A PSYCHOTYPE? 1

HISTRIONICS 16

EPILEPTOIDS 70

HYPERTHYMICS 135

CONFORMALS 163

SCHIZOIDS 179

NARCISSISTICS & FANATICS 209

EMOTIVES 249

RHAPSODICS 260

HYPOTHYMICS 292

EPILOGUE 318

BIBLIOGRAPHY 323

1

What is a Psychotype?

"Character is both formed and revealed by how one deals with everyday situations as well as extraordinary pressures and temptations. Like a well-made tower, character is built stone by stone, decision by decision"

(Michael Josephson)

Have you ever thought about why people act the way they do? Why do some people stubbornly insist on being right while they are obviously wrong? Why do some people enjoy gathering attention towards themselves? Why do some employers never show any admiration whatsoever, regardless of how well your performance is? Why are some people judgemental against you? Why have these people, though they do not know you, decided not to like you? And most importantly, why cannot you understand and manage these people's behavior, and develop a strong relationship with them?

Psychotypes

For quite a long time, these questions remained unanswered. They were considered the kind always to linger around, reminding us of how some areas are mysteries after all. However, you will find the answers to all these questions in this book and a lot more along with it.

When you meet someone new, you will be able to know almost anything about their character. You will learn how to structure your behavior, speech and character to communicate with people in the most effective manner possible. You will ensure that when you speak, people listen. You will know how to keep their attention on you and transform that attention into admiration.

While reading this book, you will revisit your relationships with everyone in your life. You will understand the reasons behind all their actions and decisions. You will understand why people are the way they are and how you can use this knowledge for your own benefit or the benefit of others.

I will teach you something new to achieve these targets – something that you have never seen or have read before. We are going to learn the ***psychotypes***. Mastery over psychotypes will allow you to communicate with others elegantly and effectively since you will be learning their psychological language. If you do not use the psycholanguage of the person in front of you, they may fail to understand you. They may even oppose you. Shamans have an old saying:

"The reason why you keep asking yourself 'why this always keeps happening to me' is that the lesson continues until you learn"

Most of our interactions with people do not yield favorable results because we do not know if we made a mistake somewhere. And because we do not know whether something we did was a mistake, we eventually end up repeating it. And sometimes, we fail because we miss the opportunities to strengthen our relationships. By learning the characters of various people, you will easily notice when such opportunities present themselves, and you will know exactly how to seize them. Building any form of a social relationship, whether personal or professional, will be as easy for you as it gets.

Learning psychotypes has a lot more merits than effective communication and building strong relationships. This field will help you to influence, negotiate, persuade, lead, and even manipulate people. It will help you to be liked, adored, and respected by others, and people will be much more likely to comply with your requests. If you master this field, you will ensure that others listen and even obey while you speak. You will succeed because you'll know what the person in front of you wants to hear or see. You'll be a step ahead of everyone.

For example, if you're dealing with histrionics, giving them what they want would only backfire as it leads to their disinterest. The most they crave is attention, and when you give these people what they want, they eventually move on to wanting something else. Hence, it is essential you provide them with just enough attention to please them once in a while but not more than that.

But the most important contribution of learning psychotypes will be *"self-actualization"*. Every person in the world has to have full knowledge, command and control over himself. He needs to be fully aware of his thought process, behavior, character, potential, and all the possibilities that come with it. We have to understand in which conditions we thrive and in which we do not. We need to understand whether we are suited for areas requiring creativity or standard thinking. For all this, we need to understand our psychotype and be fully aware of ourselves.

What is a Psychotype?

10 Main Psychotypes

The reactions you show to your surroundings depend directly on your nature, that is, your character. If we analyze people carefully, it can be seen that everybody has unique functions in the community. Character plays an essential role in forming these functions. Our character is formed through genetic and social factors.

1) Genetic transfer of the character is the transfer of the mother's and father's character to the child.

2) The social development of the character is developed based on the social atmosphere, including family upbringing, school, university, friends, and professional life. M. Josephson's quote illustrates this point.

In this book, we interchangeably use the concepts of "character" and "psychotype". That is to say, they are the same. There are ten main psychotypes, and every one of us possesses some of the traits from each psychotype. However, one of these psychotypes is more dominant in our behavior than the rest. But sometimes, we may dominantly resemble the traits of more than one psychotype. This is called *'branching'*.

For example, assume a genetic schizoid branches with a fanatic psychotype. In this situation, his character will strongly improve, i.e., his self-consciousness and emotional intelligence will increase substantially. Schizoids naturally lack self-care and discipline, their emotional intelligence is weak, while quite the opposite is true for fanatics. As such, when we branch with another psychotype, we tend to strengthen our character, reduce the natural weaknesses imposed by our genetic psychotype and overall, become a richer personality. Branching of psychotypes can occur only through the social development of the character, e.g., education, family upbringing, life experiences and so on.

Now, let's look at the definition of each of the ten psychotypes:

Histrionics – these people crave attention and thus, act in an extravagant and exhibitionist manner. Having huge ego, superficiality and shallowness are among their core character traits.

Epileptoids – these people are tough, stiff and severe. They reduce their lives to systematic formats and demand others to follow their rules and plans.

Hyperthymics – these people enjoy an active life, and they perceive everything positively. They are vivacious, adventurous and mischievous. They are witty and whimsical, and they enjoy the company of like-minded individuals.

Conformals – imitation and dependence on immediate surroundings. These people fall under peer influence, and they tend to think and act like their friends and comrades.

Schizoids – these people possess an unusual attitude towards life. They value independence more than anything and they avoid all commitments and responsibilities. They are not organized, accurate or tidy. Instead, they are messy, chaotic and very clumsy. These people are daydreamers and possess a rich fantasy world. Eccentricity is among their core personality traits.

Narcissistics – these are healthy narcissists who are self-confident, respectful of others, and target-oriented. They are skillful and talented and fight for their values and principles. You will learn to distinguish between a narcissist, a personality disorder, and a narcissistic psychotype.

Fanatics – these people have strong inner power, leadership skills, and global and wide-scaled goals. Their lives have been built on principles and values that they believe serve the greater good.

Emotives – sensitive to their environment. They prefer listening to others by sharing their sorrow. They are selfless and can sacrifice their comfort for others.

Rhapsodics – also known as psychasthenics. These people love a safe life. They usually panic and feel the symptoms of stress and always prefer being careful. They follow the philosophy *"look before you leap"* or *"better safe than sorry"*.

Hypothymics – these people live a passive and monotonous life. They approach everything in a critical manner. They put logic over emotionality. They are also highly introverted.

The Nervous System

The nervous system is one of the determining factors of our psychotype. Your nervous system will have a direct impact on your character, and hence, on your personality. In this book, the nervous system will not be studied scientifically because there is another field called *"neuroscience"* – the branch of science studying the nervous system. What we will do is to study the impact of the nervous system on human character.

What is a Psychotype?

The nervous system is categorized according to its speed and strength in order to observe human behavior. For example, people with a fast nervous system reach conclusions very quickly. They do not put in enough time to process things through. As such, they have a superficial and shallow attitude.

So, our character is strongly affected by our nervous system. For instance, histrionics, rhapsodics, and hyperthymics often blunder because they often speak without thinking. This is because they have a fast nervous system. Due to their fast nervous system, they do not take time to process information before responding. For example, they do not develop an inner dialogue to analyze information. They avoid details, and hence, their responses appear superficial. The fast nervous system makes them impatient as well.

On the other hand, epileptoids and narcissistics have a gradual nervous system. This means that they gradually process information before responding. For this reason, they have a strong inner dialogue, they are argumentative, and they think in detail. They are also patient and take time when working on projects.

Then there is the strength of the nervous system. In this book, we will use the strength of the nervous system to determine whether a person is resilient, works well under crisis, and has a strong control of his emotions. For example, hyperthymics and narcissistics have a strong nervous system. That is why they have strong self-confidence. They do not lose their heads when facing criticisms. On the other hand, histrionics, epileptoids and rhapsodics have a weak nervous system. That is why, when criticized, they get extremely emotional and genuinely offended.

Personality Disorders

What do you think the *"accentuation of character"* means? It is a condition when our character traits strengthen. It is not necessarily a bad thing as it could mean that the positive traits of character are strengthening. But there is also something known as *"pathological accentuation of character"*. If I ask you the same question now, you will probably say that it means nothing good.

And you are right. As the name suggests, the pathological accentuation of character is when certain traits of your personality have strengthened to a degree where they have become extreme, e.g., abnormal, unhealthy, irrational and so on. Simply, pathological accentuation of character becomes the ground for acute reactions, which is a condition for the development of personality disorders!

What is a Psychotype?

There can be multiple reasons why any person may develop a certain personality disorder, and pathological accentuation of our character or our psychotype is one of them. In this book, you'll learn every one of the main psychotypes and the personality disorder arising from its pathological accentuation. At the end of some chapters, I have added the brief section called *"Pathological Accentuation of the Psychotype"*, briefly studying the **DSM** and **ICD** equivalent personality disorder for each psychotype. This means that you will also be introduced to the field of clinical psychology.

- **DSM:** *Diagnostic and Statistical Manual of Mental Disorders (by the American Psychiatric Association)*

- **ICD:** *International Classification of Diseases (by the World Health Organization)*

Note that some psychotypes do not experience pathological accentuation, such as hyperthymics and emotives. Also, some disorders are unlikely to be caused by pathological accentuation, such as cyclothymia, bipolar disorder, schizoid personality disorder, borderline personality disorder, etc. The personality disorders that are unlikely to be caused through the pathological accentuation of psychotype will not be studied in this book.

But it is useful to know why a person may develop a certain personality disorder, apart from the pathological accentuation of his character. Let me briefly provide some reasons here:

1) Diseases (brain injuries, infections, intoxication, psychotraumas, and so on)

2) Congenital neural system inferiority due to heredity, birth injury, etc.

3) Social reasons (being a victim of bullying, treason, unfaithfulness, etc.)

Now, how would you distinguish between a psychotype or personality disorder? To be precise, let's take a person who resembles histrionic traits. How would you know if this person is only a member of the histrionic psychotype or has the histrionic personality disorder? I am confident to say that it will become apparent and very natural as you make your way through this book. But it will be useful at this stage to say that a personality disorder usually satisfies the following conditions:

1) The character remains relatively stable throughout life

2) The features of the character are extreme and obvious

3) The person constantly faces life difficulties

4) The same traits of character are monotonous everywhere, e.g., if a man is a despot at home but friendly outside, he is not a psychopath since he can adjust his behavior per his environment

Individuals with personality disorders are clients of psychiatrists, and they require careful attention and care. Such conditions should be carried out and treated only by professionals. Please, do not embark on treating such disorders after getting courageous from reading this book.

Last but not the least, the character may exhibit itself secretly or obviously. Although character shows itself secretly in people with no mental disorders, it becomes evident in psychopathologic cases. Such people are psychologically vulnerable.

For example, suppose you take the cell phone of an epileptoid. If he makes a polite protest and asks for his phone back, he probably has a healthy character accentuation with no signs of psychopathy. However, if he gets impolite, angry or even threatens you, his character might have accentuated to a pathological level, and he should seek medical help.

Final remarks

Before concluding, I need you not to confuse the personality with psychotype. It is common to confuse these concepts. Psychotype is a crucial component of personality, but it is not all of the personality. Personality is much richer because it includes our psychotype, discipline, intellect, skills and capabilities, habits and dependencies, hobbies and phobias, morals and values, intentions and goals, social status and birth status, ideology, worldview, and many more. For this reason, our personality is richer, though our psychotype will dictate our behavior.

Classifying people to psychotypes requires paying attention to several traits. Almost in all chapters, you will usually have the following subchapters:

1) Thought process (including the nervous system)

2) Behavior

3) External Appearance

4) Emotional State (including mimicry and gesticulations)

5) Social Relationships

What is a Psychotype?

However, each psychotype is unique, and for that reason, there will be some deviations from the structure above, i.e., in some psychotypes, there will be certain subchapters that will not appear in others. For example, the subchapter *"My Choice"* appears only when studying the histrionic psychotype, while *"Dysphoria and Explosiveness"* will appear only in epileptoids.

Furthermore, you will learn valuable techniques of manipulation, influence, and seduction as you read through the chapters that are highly applicable to anyone. But what is more, you will also learn the specific manipulation techniques for each psychotype. This way, you will be able to tailor the best influence tools for every individual you will meet in your life.

Now we can start learning about each psychotype individually. Get ready to enjoy!

2

Histrionics

"Looking good isn't self-importance; it's self-respect"

(Charles Hix)

This quote is used to envision the character type for which the external appearance is of paramount importance. Indeed, such people belong to none other than the histrionic psychotype. Histrionics love being under the spotlight and having a stylish lifestyle. They **behave demonstratively since they crave attention**. When talking to them, you can feel artificiality and over sociability in their behavior. Histrionics also love talking loudly. All these behaviors of histrionics stem directly from their need for attention. William Shakespeare, the prominent English playwright and poet, has said:

"All the world's a stage, and all the men and women merely players"

Histrionics

The word "histrionic" comes from the Latin word "histrio", which translates into an "actor". As if Shakespeare used these words to describe the character of histrionics since they behave in such a demonstrative and figurative manner that makes others think that they are acting. Histrionics were named as such due to their theatrical and exhibitionist behaviors. Such character features are most often attributed to females, specifically sassy and self-absorbed females, like the sorority girls or cheerleaders that we often see in American TV series.

When studying any psychotype, you must start with a clear picture of their behavior. For histrionics, the concept of *"self-importance"* is the most essential. Very often, histrionics possess the narcissistic traits as well. For example, a histrionic professes to be an indispensable part of society, as though everything that happens is or should be about him.

Furthermore, due to the high feeling of self-importance, histrionics feel entitled towards all merits of life, such as attention, care, gifts, money, approval and admiration. If such thoughts are not amended before adulthood, then the delusionality, grandiosity and lack of self-reflection will be among the most fundamental traits of a histrionic's character.

In such conditions, the character may accentuate to a pathological state, and the individual may end up with a histrionic personality disorder.

Histrionics are hedonistic because self-indulgence has the utmost importance for them. Also, they feel like it is their right to enjoy everything that life has to offer – another trait arising from an elevated feeling of self-importance. As such, histrionics are highly self-interested and often selfish. Their main philosophy could be written as "unrestricted pursuit of self-interest".

For example, the attention-craving behavior of histrionics is directly related to their feeling of self-importance and hedonism since attention is a pleasure stimulant. As you can deduce, histrionics love compliments and flattery. Additionally, histrionics often resemble strong narcissistic traits due to the elevated feelings of self-importance, self-interest and grandiosity.

Now that you have learned the fundamental personality traits of histrionics, let's dig deeper into their thought process. Note that, the nervous system of histrionics is weak. As such, they lack resilience and cannot tolerate criticisms. Additionally, their nervous system is fast, implying that they come to conclusions very quickly. But on the downside, they are superficial and shallow.

Thought Process

Histrionics prefer to live and interact figuratively and demonstratively. They often exhibit provocative and seductive behavior to incite interest during contact. This behavior leads others to view them theatrically. They have special appearance that attract attention and distinguish them from others. It is very easy to become a victim of histrionics' lies as they live in a great fantasy. It is your utmost responsibility to make fact-checks when listening to these people.

I would like to give an example. Donald Trump has a histrionic psychotype combined with some narcissistic traits. He enjoys being at the center of attention. As a histrionic, he has an intense fantasy and frequently makes things up. This comes directly from histrionic's fast-nervous system. Additionally, it is alleged that he told over 10,000 lies throughout his presidency.

He almost always says that people are impressed by him, e.g., during his 1st election, he said he met President Putin and that *"Putin said that I am a genius"*. This comes from histrionic's pompous behavior. He later publicly retracted these statements after the FBI investigation.

Or take when he banned people entering the U.S. from Muslim countries. He said that several NATO leaders have called and congratulated him on his decision. This comes from his need for praise, approval and validation. But when asked to name at least one of these leaders, he avoided the question. One might think it would have been a politically wrong decision to disclose names, but this is the gentleman who has been in constant handshake struggle with other world leaders and has called them names, such as *"Little Rocket Man"*.

Histrionics contrive ideas in a very short period of time; hence, we can see inconsistencies in their stories. What is the reason behind this? It is directly linked to them having a fast and weak nervous system. The fast nervous system causes them to contrive ideas in a very short period of time. However, since their nervous system is also weak, they are vulnerable to having inconsistencies in their stories. Namely, they can do something fast but cannot evaluate the details. They can answer perfunctorily to everything but cannot go into the specifics about it. This shows that they have a superficial and careless attitude.

But rhapsodics also have a weak and fast nervous system. Yet, it is not often that we observe inconsistencies in their stories. So, you might ask, if it is the weak and fast nervous system that causes histrionics to make stuff up, why is such behavior not observed in rhapsodics as well? Well, the answer is related to the behaviour of histrionics. Histrionics need attention, admiration and approval. They want people to find them cool, smart and interesting. If they do not have good stories that make them look fascinating, then they make them up. Rhapsodics, in contrast, do not feel the need to appear as captivating to others.

So, a histrionic can come up with assertions very quickly. However, when asked to support his assertions on argumentation, facts, and sources, he will pretend that it is unnecessary and will try to escape that line of questioning.

In my future book on manipulation, I will discuss how to affect the belief systems of humans. There are five main techniques to manipulate beliefs. One of them is called *"credibility"*. This technique consists of 5 sub-techniques that attacks one's credibility:

1) **Source**: what is the source of the information or thesis presented?

2) **Authors**: who authored or supported this information or thesis?

3) **Facts**: are there any facts or common knowledge that support this information?

4) **Relevance:** is the information or answer presented relevant to the question?

5) **Applicability:** is the given information or answer applicable in practice?

Credibility is a highly effective method that many professionals employ in their daily lives. It lets you cast doubt on the reliability of information supplied by someone. This technique is widely used by defense attorneys and prosecutors when questioning witnesses or interrogating the accused. It is also commonly employed by journalists and politicians.

To manipulate histrionics when they talk, it suffices to attack them from credibility. For example, since their nervous system is fast, they would not be able to reason their thoughts on argumentation. Hence, asking them about the author, source or relevance of the information will rattle them. I would like to give a personal example for this one.

When I moved into my new apartment in London, I met my neighbours in one of our common residential areas. One histrionic joined us and started to babble about his achievements, i.e., that he is a top graduate from Cambridge, doing top-notch research in cancer medication, and so on. Of course, in the presence of such powerful lies, it is tough for a profiler to sit on his hands. After asking just a few questions that he must have known if he actually did what he was talking about, such as who was the head of cancer research at Cambridge, he got rattled and embarrassed since he felt exposed.

When I was teaching *"Investment Banking"* at King's College London, I asked my students which books have helped nourish their interest in the field. One histrionic gentleman replied: *"Investments, by Bodie, Kane and Marcus"*. Since this book is an advanced textbook for postgraduate courses in finance, I was impressed and asked him:

- What did you think about their observation of increases in pension fund liabilities in 2012 in the U.S.? Do you think those funds could have reduced their exposure by following an attractive liability-driven investment strategy?

When I asked this question about the book, he was struck and could not answer. Then he admitted: *"it is not necessary for me what is written in that book. The most important thing is that when somebody asks me what book I read, I can give the name of Bodie, Kane and Marcus with great pleasure"*. This indicates histrionic's superficial character; even though they want to be informed, they cannot go into the details.

Histrionics may be smart, but when pressed to clarify their views and communicate in detail, they will be unable to do so. This is because of their fast nervous system. It prevents them from detail-oriented thinking and delegating their thoughts in an accurate manner.

We continuously face this feature of histrionics. They can talk with you about any topic even if they do not have any resources for discussion. If you ask them about economics, they will throw around random information on micro and macroeconomics. But if you ask them about the specifics or details, they would not be able to answer it.

Interestingly, they pretend as if the details are unnecessary. In this regard, you can always observe considerable superficiality and shallowness, and yet, vast erudition in histrionics.

Behavior and External Appearance

To understand histrionic's nature, never forget their attention-seeking behavior. This turns them into exhibitionists – people who act and behave extravagantly to attract attention. Being an exhibitionist goes in line with histrionics having a huge ego and being delusional.

Later, you will study egocentric and altruistic histrionics. Altruistic histrionics are aware of their insecurities, but egocentric histrionics not only suppress their insecurities but are also in denial. They respond aggressively to any comment or criticism on their behavior.

The behaviour of histrionics is based on "me", which is the reason for their exhibitionist behaviors. Do not forget that every action they take and every word they speak directly or indirectly aims to maximize their welfare. Even the selflessness of histrionics is often backed up with their future expected payoffs. For example, if a histrionic lady acts selflessly by taking care of her husband, then there is a great probability that she will ask for something in return soon. In this retrospect, histrionics are and can be manipulative. By acting selflessly, they intend to trigger the *reciprocity rule.*

This rule dictates that if one receives favor from another, they are more likely to oblige to their request in the future, even if the request is much more sizable than the initial favor.

We can often see histrionics employing the *rejection then retreat* technique. The first step in this tactic is to ask for a significant favour, one that is likely to be declined. Once rejected, then one would retreat to a smaller request, which is the request that he wanted from the start. For example, if you ask your father to allow you for a field trip with your high school friends for the whole weekend, he will say no (at least this is what my father did). But after some time, if you approach him and ask to spend your Saturday with some friends, he will be much more likely to say yes. Histrionics often employ this towards people if the initial request is rejected.

The reason that the *"rejection then retreat"* technique works very well has three reasons (*Cialdini, 1984*):

1) **Contrast Principle**: if request A that was initially asked is considerable and was rejected, then request B, which was the request retreated towards to, will seem relatively insignificant, though it might not be insignificant at all when analyzed in a pure perspective. This concept is also studied in psychophysics.

2) **Satisfaction**: the person who rejected offer A feels satisfaction after offer B is requested since they assume they have negotiated a great discount.

3) **Responsibility**: the person who rejected offer A feels responsibility for offer B being requested since their rejection led to a retreat towards a smaller request.

Histrionics have a provocative nature, especially egocentric histrionics. Their desire to provoke others and create conflict is substantial. They do so to attract attention. That being said, histrionics use all opportunities, positive or negative, to exhibit themselves. Note that they can be capricious and vindictive. That is why, be careful when sharing your secrets with them, as it is effortless for these people to create conflicts.

The members of this psychotype like provoking people, and they are pretty good at it. Assume you are talking about a topic that you are considerably good at in the environment of friends. Everyone around is impressed and follows you very attentively. In such instances, histrionics get out of control simply because you have made yourself the object of attention and have left nothing on the table for them. At this point, they can easily approach you to start a conflict. I suggest you ignore them if this happens.

Histrionics love an active life and wear fashionably. In fact, they wear whatever they can to be distinguished from others. Because dressing is important for them, they usually pay much attention to how others are dressed. They respect those who dress fashionably and want to befriend them. As such, histrionics tend to judge a book by its cover. Accompanied with their fast nervous system and superficial attitude, a histrionic being judgemental and hasty with conclusions does not come up as a surprise.

Among all people, histrionics are the ones that rely on their rules of thumbs, e.g., *"if one wears fashionably, then we will get along just well"*. That is why, histrionics are usually impulsive and irresponsible in their social lives, and they have a hard time establishing meaningful, long-term relationships. It is very easy for them to become best friends with someone and become enemies a week later.

Usually, when we arrive at social gatherings, we expect others to welcome us so that we can adapt to the environment. When someone new arrives at a party, histrionics quickly observe them and decide whether they want to meet this person or not.

This results from their judgemental behavior. The saddest part is that the victim, who was denied the "blessing" to meet the fancy histrionic, will probably think something is wrong with him. However, one should never forget that this is the nature of histrionics: if you do not outshine, they will likely ignore you.

Histrionics will not approach someone they are not interested in. For this reason, always wait for histrionics to approach you, not the other way around. Also, if you have communicated with them, and you observe even the slightest chance that they got uninterested in you, be the one to end the conversation immediately. Show them that it is you who is no longer interested. The most effective way is to interrupt them and say something like: *"Hey, I think I just saw Jamie. I will catch up with you later"*. Such a response will cause slight discomfort for a histrionic because you have left her to meet someone else.

To sum up, do not push it if a histrionic does not like you because the more you chase them, the more uninteresting you become. The best way to get their attention would be to slightly ignore them and get involved with other people around you. Try to be the focus of the group. This way, you will be attracting attention, which histrionic thrives for.

Histrionics have active, dynamic, and volatile facial expressions. These people act demonstratively. Observing their gestures, facial expressions, and even their voice tone reminds us of an actor. You can always see a sensor smile on their faces. A sensor smile is basically a fake smile. To find out if a person is histrionic or not, you have to pay attention to their facial expressions. You can usually observe flirtatious, provocative, vivacious and seductive expressions on their faces.

Histrionics

Interestingly, histrionics can freely rule their emotional reactions, e.g., they can cry for a bit, and after a few seconds, they can change their behavior and start laughing depending on the context. This behavior is very apparent in children histrionics.

When I was eight years old, I played cards with my histrionic cousin, who was a year or two younger. At one point, I caught him cheating and took the cards and threw them on his face. He started crying very loudly for our parents to hear it. He acted as such in purpose so that he could play the victim while I would get all the punishment. I immediately offered him to play Grand Theft Auto San Andreas on my computer only if he kept his mouth shut. He instantaneously agreed, wiped his eyes, and sat behind the computer with a "Grinch" smile on his face.

The rapid emotional shifts are not limited to young histrionics but to adult histrionics as well. The rapid changes in moods and wellbeing, also, the dynamic of their facial expressions, can lead others to think that histrionics are fake.

For example, assume that you have recently broken up with your boyfriend and you feel pretty bad about it. You go to the house of your friend, who also appears to be a histrionic, and you share your sorrow with her. Then suddenly, your friend's roommate approaches you both and excitedly informs you that her boyfriend proposed. Suddenly, your histrionic friend forgets about your break-up and talks only about her roommate's wedding.

Such behaviors lead us to think that histrionics are not genuine friends. But now you understand that such behavior is not related to whether they are genuine or not. It is due to the rapid changes in their emotional states caused by their fast nervous system.

Assume in such a situation, you confront your friend and say: *"what you did was very disrespectful, you have not cared for me at all! How could your emotions change so quickly? I cannot believe it!"*. In this case, you will be taking a risk because they might either emphasize with you or ignore you completely. They might even get angry at you for treating them unfairly.

Importance of "My Choice" and Annihilation Technique

For histrionics, the idea of *"my life, my choices"* is of paramount importance. They do not tolerate when someone speaks for them, makes their decisions for them, or patronizes them. Even if some histrionics have a dependant nature, like altruistic histrionics, they will only accept to hear others' advice. They will always want to make the final decision themselves.

I assume many of you have watched or are about to watch the infamous American TV series called *"How to Get Away with Murder"*. In that series, the character Michaela Pratt is a typical histrionic (with narcissistic tendencies). If you have access to Netflix, please watch season 5, episode 2. In that episode, two specific scenes from 8:40 to 9:00 and 17:30 to 18:20 represent the behavior of a histrionic discussed here. See how frustrated she becomes when Prof. Keating shifts the trial strategy without discussing it with her first.

For those who are not keen to put the book aside and watch that episode, let me provide the background story on what is happening there. Prof. Keating is a law professor who shares her own trial cases with her students so that they can get a trial experience before graduation. She chose Michaela Pratt to represent one of her clients in a murder case. But at one point, the professor decided to shift the case strategy. And Ms. Pratt, irritatingly, responds: *"This is my case, and I have not approved any changes in the strategy"*. Prof. Keating responds with: *"Well, then it is a good thing that I do not need your approval"*. And at this point, Ms. Pratt responds: *"I am not Bonnie. I am not going to sit back and let you bully me"*. Ms. Bonnie was the previous associate of Prof. Keating. Prof. Keating responds: *"There is a difference between bullying and teaching"*. Ms. Pratt interrupts with: *"The difference that you clearly do not understand. That is why Bonnie left you. That is everybody is leaving you…"*. At this moment, Prof. Keating interrupts with: *"You know what? You keep talking to me like that, and you will see what a real bully looks like"*.

For those of you who watched the episode or read the background story above, was there anything interesting that you noticed in the behavior of Ms. Pratt? Michaela Pratt assumes complete control of the case and speaks in a way as if it was her who recruited the client, did all the paperwork and wrote the appeal. But the case is part of a class-action lawsuit filed by Professor Keating in the first place. The professor chose Michaela Pratt among all students to help with the case and gain experience as an attorney before graduation, not to embarrass her publicly.

So, an outburst of this kind against Prof. Keating can be thought to be unfair, foolish, and arrogant. But such outbursts are very natural to histrionics. Once you give them even a small control over something, they will act as if it totally belongs to them. They will restrict your say in that matter, and you will never be able to regain full control of the situation by asking them nicely. This feature is also frequently observed in epileptoids.

Once this has happened, what should you do? Well, to regain control and to maintain order, that is, to prevent such behavior from happening again, there are multiple techniques that will guarantee success. However, all require professional training or natural talent since they all are combative. Here, however, I will give you one of my own techniques called *"annihilation"* so that if you ever fall into such a situation, you can restore control and manifest dominance.

Read the background story provided or watch the second scene again, where Michaela Pratt starts disrespecting Prof. Keating in front of the entire class. Prof. Keating's response was:

"You know what? You keep talking to me like that, and you will see what a real bully looks like"

Such a response is interesting but very insufficient. The following response, based on the annihilation technique, would have been more effective:

- One more outburst of this nature, *Ms. Pratt*, and let alone never having a case to work on, you will also be permanently suspended from my class. Is that understood?

Why is this response much better than Prof. Keating's response? Let us analyze in detail, word by word. To begin with, note that this sentence has five parts:

1) "*One more outburst of this nature*" ⇒ **Accusing Guilt** ⇒ is the part where you accuse your soon-to-be-annihilated victim of their adverse behavior. This part is very important because it will silence the person in front of you, and they will not disturb you until you finish your word.

2) "*Ms. Pratt*" ⇒ **Addressing the Victim** ⇒ is the part where you call out the name of the person. It comes after *"Accusing Guilt"* but before the *"Hidden Threat"*. Addressing someone with their name triggers *positive recognition*. In this case, it will increase the fear of the

person since he automatically becomes more attentive to a potential threat once his name is called. When the awareness to a threat increases, the subconscious mind tells that the threat is real and potentially dangerous.

3) *"Let alone never having a case to work on again"* ⟹ **Hidden Threat** ⟹ is perhaps the most important part of the annihilation technique. This part comes before annihilation. It strengthens the severity of the situation and makes the actual threat that will be made in the next part appear much severe. The hidden threat must be *context-dependent*. For example, in the case of Keating v. Pratt, the dispute began because Ms. Pratt overstepped the line by saying that *"This is my case, and I have not approved any changes in the strategy"*. Now we know the reason for her irritation ⟹ *"my case"*. So, threatening her that she will never have any case again with such behavior will shake her from the very core.

4) *"You will also be permanently suspended from my class"* ⟹ **Annihilation** ⟹ this is where you annihilate your victim. This part intends to make your victim realize that they could lose a lot more than the case at hand. Also, it

supports the next part, *"Realization"*, since the victim thinks that if they received such a large threat, then perhaps they were very disrespectful in the first place.

5) *"Is that understood?"* $\Rightarrow$ **Realization** $\Rightarrow$ you pose a question that is not intended to be answered. This leads to a mental trance by creating feelings of guilt, shame, and fear.

So, histrionics would not allow anyone to interfere with their choices. But what lies behind this principle? Why are they so insecure about losing control? The reason behind this is actually admirable: histrionics cannot allow themselves to appear weak. This is a trait of a leader!

But histrionics should note that the true leader knows his bounds, never challenges someone stronger. Never outshine the master – the first law of power in Robert Greene's infamous book *"48 Laws of Power"*. Michaela Pratt made that huge mistake. If you hit your master to knock him down, you better make sure that he does not get back up.

I would like to give another example. On one of the day-offs, my ex-colleague was invited to a friend's home. His friend's father, who was a member of epileptoid psychotype, asked him the following question:

- *During our arguments, he starts defending himself aggressively and he does so by raising his voice. After a while, he makes jokes and talks as if nothing has happened. How can you explain that?*

- *Your son is a histrionic, and histrionics show resistance during disputes because they do not want to look weak. This process lasts for a short time. Even if the members of this psychotype want to look strong, their inner strength is weaker than those of the fanatics, narcissistics and epileptoids. Hence, histrionics belong to a weak psychotype category.*

Another example, when journalists criticize Mr. Trump, he gets aggressive instantaneously because it directly affects his ego. He ignores questions asked to him and answers irrelevantly and mostly attacks the one who asked the question. Indeed, ***ignore*** and ***deception*** are among the frequent manipulation techniques in the armory of histrionics.

Social Relationships

As you might already know, histrionics have strong sense of self-importance. They perform tactical steps both in their professional and personal lives to get ahead and be differentiated. Furthermore, they are innovative, in contrast to epileptoids, rhapsodics, and emotives. When performing a task, they are the ones who emerge with alternative solutions. Because a histrionic believes that she has a unique and exciting life, she believes that those who oppose her are naive. After all, they have no idea how privileged they are to be in her presence.

Histrionics think positively about themselves. They love being praised and differentiated, and they do their best for it. Their speech starts and ends with "me". To look active and talented, they set their speech fast and demonstratively. They may tell you about their career, family, or the accident that occurred to them in a matter of minutes. A histrionic's communication, which entails moving from one point to another, is an act they perform flawlessly. This is something they have in common with hyperthymics. These people are creative enough to think of many new ideas in a matter of seconds, but they prefer to assign them to others to execute. For this reason, their leadership skills do not develop completely. They are attractive and creative enough to inspire others for a given task, but they cannot get into the details of work due to their fast and nervous system.

Histrionics love to manipulate others to achieve their own goals. For example, a histrionic lady in your school can all of a sudden pay attention to you, invite you over for a coffee, or even start flirting with you. Once you succumb to her charms, she may ask you to assist her, most likely by taking on and managing some of her responsibilities. When I was an undergraduate, one of my smart friends at King's College London was affected by one histrionic lady's beauty. However, she was not interested in having a relationship with my friend. Nonetheless, she usually flirted with him a week or two before exams. And later, she would ask him for help to prepare for the exams.

Now, if you compliment a histrionic, they will embrace it genuinely and be affected by it, but if you do the same with an epileptoid, they will begin wondering if you have a hidden agenda. Although histrionics can be influenced easily, they are good at influencing others too. If they want to go to a cinema with you, they will do their best to make you cancel or delay your existing plans and commitments. This usually happened to my poor friend at KCL when that lady manipulated him (he was trying to reschedule his meetings with me and others).

Histrionics enjoy surprises. Once, my girlfriend prepared a romantic dinner by decorating the whole place with candles and turning off the lights. When I rang the doorbell, she opened the door excitedly and said: *"surprise! Baby"*. For some reason, the schizoid part of my brain was more dominant (schizoids lack intuition), and I responded: *"please do not tell me that lights are off? I was hoping to watch XYZ"*. Of course, it killed all her motivation, and I ended up sleeping on the couch (but at least I could Netflix all night, though the "chill" part was missing). All in all, I had to "bust my ass" the next day to make it up to her.

When histrionic's wishes are not realized, they get out of control. They are obsessed with things they cannot have. I have previously stated not to give them what they want straight away. Because the more inaccessible something is, the more obsessed a histrionic will get on it. This can be you; that is, if a histrionic wants you, tease her a lot, do not surrender quickly. Although you may desire her a lot, you should always hide your intentions. Histrionics love mystery. The more they cannot understand your intentions, the more passionate they will become about you.

How to Charm Histrionics: "Seduction" Technique

The discussion of social relationships of histrionics leads us to a manipulation technique called "*seduction*". There are several ways in which you may employ this technique. I personally use it differently for each psychotype. I intend to teach you how to employ this technique on histrionics since most people want to engage in romantic relationships with the members of this psychotype due to their attractiveness and popularity.

How do you tailor the seduction technique towards histrionics? Remember, histrionics get obsessed over things they cannot get. You have to seduce them through this channel. I intend to teach you this technique in an applied manner. What I will do is to give a real-life example taken from 17th century France. I came across this story in Robert Greene's book: *"48 Laws of Power"*. Let me start by giving you the history of events that happened.

Story of one Marquis de Sevigné: Have you ever heard of Anne "Ninon" de l'Enclos? She was an XVII century French author and patron of the arts. What is more interesting, she was an infamous courtesan. She was involved with notable and wealthy lovers, such as the king's cousin Great Condé. When she encountered marquis, she had already mastered the art of love, while marquis was 22 years old and very inexperienced. Marquis approached Ninon, for he had succumbed to the charms of a beautiful but difficult young countess. Marquis told her that he chased the countess continuously, but the countess never responded favourably. Ninon decided to help him win over this gorgeous lady.

Case: Ninon taught marquis to restart his relationship with the countess, approach her and start from zero. Later, Ninon would teach marquis the techniques to seduce the countess:

1) To start from zero, approach the countess and engage in communication while keeping a measurable distance.

2) The next time you are alone with the countess, convince her that you are genuinely interested in her as a friend, not as a lover.

3) At the next encounter, a party in Paris, show up with a beautiful young woman and ensure that she brings equally beautiful female friends.

4) Ninon directed marquis not to attend those parties and gatherings where the countess expected to see him. While simultaneously, she directed marquis to attend to

those affairs where the countess frequently attended but never expected to see him.

Now, your task is to read through all four steps in the preceding instance and, to the best of your knowledge, intuition, and instincts on histrionics and manipulative techniques, clearly define their purposes: why are they effective and with which channels do they seduce the countess. This question is not intended to challenge your knowledge, rather employ your logic.

Solution: Now, we will firstly outline each step and then give the intended purpose of seduction:

1) To start from zero, approach the countess and engage in communication while keeping a measurable distance.

Intended Purpose for Seduction: it is important to start from zero so the countess forgets her previous picture of marquis that would be undesirable for seducing her. It is also important to keep a measurable distance from her in this meeting to seem casual and indifferent towards the countess. This will help to start from zero and ease the execution of step 2.

2) In the next chance, when you get the opportunity to be private with the countess, convince her that you are interested in her only as a friend, not as a lover.

Intended Purpose for Seduction: this would distract her from the marquis's purpose of seducing her. It would throw her off the scent and additionally *confuse* her. She had a picture of marquis who was desperate for her romantic attention. When histrionic ladies think this way, the affected gentleman becomes uninteresting. However, marquis confiding in her that he is not interested in a romantic relationship would somewhat remove the previous stereotype that she held on to marquis. But only if marquis continues to act in a manner that does not prove otherwise. As such, she would no longer take his interest in her for granted.

Here we have "***psychology of loss***" as well. People have a natural inclination to reclaim what they've lost, particularly if it was something they took for granted. This emotion is further amplified when it is losing someone's interest and attention. This works much stronger in histrionics.

Now that we have confused the countess and made her realize that she has lost marquis' affection, we need to move on to the third step, which is making her *jealous*. This ordering is important because in the sequence when jealousy follows confusion and psychology of loss, it creates a stronger overall effect.

In addition, marquis will employ the technique called "*social proof*" in order to exhibit himself as "desirable". The combination of "*jealousy*" and "*social proof*" will push the countess into a quest that she will enjoy – winning the Marquis de Sevigne.

> 3) At the next party, be accompanied by a beautiful, youthful lady and ensure that she brings equally beautiful girlfriends.

Intended Purpose for Seduction: previously, we collapsed all the opinions of the countess on marquis. We confused her and triggered the psychology of loss. Now is the time to make her jealous and create a ***desire to chase*** marquis.

Now, whenever the countess will turn to check up on marquis in that party, she will see him surrounded by the most stunning young ladies of Paris. In addition to jealousy, another manipulation technique is employed here – *social proof*. The countess will see that marquis is desired by other equally-attractive women – those who are perhaps even more beautiful and demanded than the countess herself.

"The idea of social proof states that one means we use to determine what is correct is to find out what other people think is correct. The principle applies especially to the way we decide what constitutes correct behavior. We view a behavior as more correct in a given situation to the degree that we see others performing it".

Quoted from: Cialdini (1984), Influence, pg. 116

Confusion and jealousy made the countess intrigued and interested in the marquis, but when there is a concept of social proof, it will trigger the countess to chase marquis. The reason is interesting: a woman interested in a man enjoys seeing that other equally attractive women are interested in him as well. This is a fixed action pattern of all human beings – something that makes us vulnerable to manipulation. Thus, social proof not only makes marquis desirable but also makes the idea of winning and snatching him away more and more satisfying.

Furthermore, we have another powerful manipulation technique that is employed here: "***element of surprise***". It was the first time countess saw marquis as desirable by other ladies. People are more likely to pay attention and think about a topic if it surprises them. More would the countess think about marquis, more will she fall to his trap. Additionally, such element of surprise helps marquis from another channel as well – the countess did not know that marquis was desirable. Hence, not only it collapses her previous judgements on marquis but also shifts them completely. As so, she will feel guilty for missing out on such an appealing gentleman. The next technique is all about employing an additional "element of surprise" to defeat the countess.

Side note*: if there are 1000 manipulation techniques available, I will venture to state that the element of surprise is one of the most powerful among them. I suggest you read the research published by Stanley Milgram and John Sabini in 1975 if you would like to learn more on how this technique works and can be applied in practice.*

4) Ninon directed marquis not to attend to those parties and gatherings where the countess expected to see him. While simultaneously, she directed marquis to attend to those affairs where the countess frequently attended but never expected to see him.

Intended Purpose for Seduction: we have the countess at the desirable state now: she got confused, she gout jealous, psychology of loss was triggered, she got caught in the element of surprise, manipulated by social proof, and now she is interested in marquis. She wants to snatch him away. What is next is to play with her even more – with the element of surprise.

When the countess goes to parties, affairs, and gatherings where marquis would usually attend, since she is already intrigued in him, she would think about meeting him before arriving there; perhaps she would even practice scripts for marquis. However, marquis not attending those meetings would disappoint her, but at the same time, intrigue her as well.

This also leads the countess to realize that the attention and company of marquis are not to be taken for granted. Since she cannot get to see the marquis even at the gatherings where he is expected to be, then he is a hard man to get to. The countess is being affected by the *scarcity*. Not to mention, scarcity is also a powerful tool of influence. On the other hand, when marquis shows up at meetings that the countess did not expect him, then such element of surprise leads to the *excitement*. She did not have the chance to meet the marquis in the previous affair, but now he is here! This does not only excite the countess; it also surprises her. She understands there is more to marquis than meets the eye.

I'm sure you're all curious as to what happened next. Did the countess fell head over heels in love with marquis?

Well, it took several weeks while marquis implemented all these things dictated by Ninon. At the same time, Ninon monitored the entire progress. From her people, she learned that the countess was falling to marquis's charms since she started to laugh harder at his jokes, she became more attentive when he spoke, and she started asking questions about the marquis from her surroundings. Ninon's team notified her that the countess would chase after marquis at all gatherings and events. Ninon was assured that the countess was under marquis's spells.

However, our dear marquis screwed up. On the next occasion, when he was at the countess's home in private, he could not keep his big fat mouth shut. He acted on his hunch with a complete disregard to Ninon's instructions. He took countess's hand and suddenly confessed his love. In this instant, all those confusions and intricacies in the countess's head were resolved. She lost her interest in marquis because she was no longer confused or intrigued. Her feelings freed themselves from marquis's charms — the end.

What should you learn from this section, apart from seducing histrionics? The key take-away would be being unattainable. Histrionics get passionately attached to those with whom they cannot be close. But this works only if you can intrigue them and lead them to a state where they are interested in chasing you. You already have a few tools in your armory to do so – tools that you learned from the description of events that happened between the Marquis de Sevigne and the young countess. Now you need to apply them – go and get it!

Types of Histrionics

Although we could classify histrionics into several subtypes, it is rather very useful to divide them into two categories: *altruistics* and *egocentrics*. Egocentric histrionics, as the name suggests, expect everyone to care for their needs, and they act as if the world revolves around them. They often resemble some narcissistic traits as well, such as the heightened feelings of self-importance. On the other hand, altruistic histrionics try to placate and appease others just to gain their attention and approval.

Egocentric histrionics always wait for others to seek them, e.g., if they become sick, they will expect others to reach out to them, care for them and be considerate. If their friends and family do not do it, they will hold a severe grudge and become very angry and rude. Nonetheless, they will calm down and forget their resentment the moment they confront you on this topic, though enduring that confrontation will not be a piece of cake. If you want it to be over as soon as possible, just ignore them.

Unlike egocentric histrionics, altruistic histrionics are appeasing, charitable and friendly. As such, they are similar to emotives. But there is a core difference. The charitability of emotives stems directly from their selfless and loving nature, while for altruistic histrionics, it stems from the rewards they will reap later. Such rewards are not necessarily materialistic. Most of the time, altruistic histrionics seek love, care and attention.

Altruistic histrionics are similar to hypothymics in the regard that they tend to exaggerate their problems. For instance, if an altruistic histrionic lives through a misfortune, even a slight one, then he will start talking about it to their friends and family in an exaggerated manner. Such minor misfortunes involve not getting what they wanted from their partners, being mistreated by a close friend, and etc. They do so purposefully – they seek to get others' attention and empathy.

Egocentric histrionics are grown up as spoilt and selfish children. Their demands have never been ignored. For this reason, they start feeling exceptional. It is vice versa for altruistic histrionics. Their parents try to humble them. We mostly face this situation when parents belong to the epileptoid psychotype. Epileptoid parents prefer raising their children with rules and discipline. But a histrionic's independent nature does not allow him to be obedient; hence, this process leads to changes in his character. Such changes include declining self-esteem, lack of independent thinking and decision-making, and becoming vulnerable to peer pressure at adolescent ages.

That is to say, the traits of conformity and dependence start increasing. As such, one of the main differences in the thought processes between egocentric and altruistic histrionics is that egocentric histrionics make their decisions independently. In contrast, altruistic histrionics often seek the approval of others.

Theodore Millon, in his 2004 book titled *"Personality Disorders in Modern Life"*, classified the histrionic personality disorder

(HPD) into six subtypes: *appeasing, theatrical, infantile, vivacious, tempestuous and disingenuous*. However, he did not provide enough detail and description for each subtype. Also, these subtypes of HPD are not recognized either by ICD or DSM. Nonetheless, the four of these subtypes are useful to know in practice. I am specifically excluding tempestuous and disingenuous histrionics as their personality features are at the level of personality disorder and cannot be viewed as character traits. You will observe that vivacious histrionics are somewhat similar to egocentric histrionics, while appeasing histrionics are akin to altruistic histrionics.

Vivacious Histrionics: Falls to the category of egocentric histrionics. These people are energetic, high-spirited, cheerful and self-confident. They are almost identical to the members of the hyperthymic psychotype. These people can also be called *"histrionics with hyperthymic tendencies"*. But unlike hyperthymics, vivacious histrionics possess an attention-seeking behavior, and for this purpose, they are seductive. Also, they are not as self-sufficient as hyperthymics. Some vivacious histrionics are grandiose and have a heightened feeling of self-importance. Their hedonistic tendencies could be damaging to others as these people lack empathy. For example, vivacious histrionics get angry with their parents if they cannot afford to buy something that they want. They could even throw a temper tantrum. As such, vivacious histrionics may resemble some narcissistic traits too.

Appeasing Histrionics: Falls to the category of altruistic histrionics. These people do not resemble the provocative behaviors of histrionics. Instead, they try their best to avoid trouble. If someone gets offended by them, they will try their best to soothe the situation. As such, they are compromising. Even the slightest of conflicts are cause for serious discomfort. This is because they do not want to lose someone's attention or admiration. They compromise themselves in an extreme manner just for approval or admiration. The members of this subtype can even sacrifice their ego and pride to bury the hatchet. In times of conflict, they tend to absorb the damage so that everyone can move on. Sometimes, their tendency to placate a conflict, which is beyond repair, reaches the level of redundancy and threatens their social image. They find it very difficult to move on from their personal relationships and are vulnerable to getting obsessed with people.

Theatrical Histrionics: These histrionics are very good-looking, self-confident and highly popular. The exhibitionist features of these histrionics are almost natural. That is to say, the way they exhibit themselves to attract attention is done in a very eloquent manner so that people usually do not view their actions and behaviors as attention-seeking. However, as with all histrionics, they act so because they crave attention. Among all histrionics, the members of this subtype are the least likely to get obsessed over others. Histrionics tend to believe that their relationships with people are more intimate than they actually are. This is one of their key character traits. However, theatrical histrionics possess this trait the least. They strongly exhibit the features of individualism and independence. Hedonism and the pursuit of self-interest in an independent manner are observed the strongest in these histrionics. The countess in the story of "Marquis de Sevigne" was a theatrical histrionic.

Infantile Histrionics: Remember when I said that the emotional state of histrionics is very rapid and dynamic. This applies to all histrionics. But this personality trait is observed more dominantly in infantile histrionics. Such histrionics are also known as "*labile histrionics*". As a personality trait, lability involves having emotions that are very dynamic, rapid, unstable, and easily stimulated. Easy stimulation of emotions is a character trait where a person's emotions can get easily aroused.

Paul Ekman argued that there are six fundamental emotions that people have. These are anger, sadness, happiness, fear, surprise and disgust. You can often observe these emotions being easily aroused in histrionics, and more frequently, in infantile histrionics. Since the emotional state of these people is extremely volatile, it can change spontaneously in any situation.

Infantile histrionics are very touchy, and it is very easy to upset them. This is because they are highly demanding – they need people to show them care and attention. In situations where the feelings of anger, sadness or disgust are heightened, infantile histrionics can get hysterical. But this type of hysteria will be almost identical to having a temper tantrum. For this reason, this lasts only for a short period of time.

Histrionic Personality Disorder

So far, we have analyzed and studied the features of the histrionic psychotype. Now we will study the pathological accentuation of this character, which usually leads to the development of **Histrionic Personality Disorder**, often abbreviated and referred to as HPD.

I cannot say this enough: do not confuse a character with a personality disorder. It might get a bit trickier since almost all traits of the HPD are present in the histrionic psychotype as well. However, there are certain things that can help you differentiate between the histrionic psychotype and the personality disorder.

To begin with, since HPD is a personality disorder, an individual diagnosed with an HPD must also be diagnosed with a General Personality Disorder (GPD). This is not something that I can teach you to do flawlessly in this book but to see whether an individual could be diagnosed with GPD, see if they exhibit some or all of the following three attributes:

1) A pervasive and maladaptive abnormal behavior

2) Enduring and long-term abnormal behavior

3) Disharmonious attitudes and behavior

It will be much easier and efficient for you to see whether a person has an HPD if you do the following. Firstly, suppose a person has traits that resemble HPD. In that case, they are not to be the clients of psychologists or psychiatrists as long as these traits have not accentuated extremely or pathologically.

It is easy to see if an accentuation of histrionic character is at the extreme – pay attention to the main 6 criteria below:

1) Is there a persistent behavior of excessive and unhealthy state of emotionality?

2) Is the degree of discomfort obvious in situations where they are not at the center of attention?

3) Is it frequent to notice inappropriate seductive behavior?

4) Is it frequent to notice inappropriate provocative behavior?

5) Is the degree of superficiality at an extreme level, such as excessive lack of detail in speech?

6) Is it often to notice a state of extreme self-dramatization?

I hope this helped you understand the pathological accentuation of character. As long as the traits of any psychotype are not extremely accentuated, then do not label them with a disorder.

Now, I would like to propose the remaining personality traits of histrionics that I have not covered so far. These are such traits that are more recognizable in the people with HPD.

HPD resembles a pattern of extreme attention-seeking and exhibitionist behaviors. The demonstration of such behaviors usually starts showing itself in early childhood. These behaviors include improper seduction and a huge desire for approval.

When studying histrionic psychotype, it was stated that rapid mood shifts cause others to see histrionics as fake, superficial, or extravagant. Such rapidly shifting emotional states are frequented in people with HPD as well.

There is another feature that people with HPD have strongly in common with members of histrionic psychotype – using factitious physical or psychological problems to attract others' attention. To be specific, both histrionics and people with HPD may talk about non-existing or insignificant life problems in an exaggerated manner in order to convince others of their tedious hardships. But they do so just to attract others' sympathy, consideration, and attention. Such behavior is known as *"Factitious disorder imposed on self"* or *"Munchausen syndrome"*. However, people with such syndrome might harm themselves for attention, though histrionics do not tend to harm themselves. But they do feign mental or physical problems just to draw attention.

Histrionics are easily influenced by others, especially those who treat them approvingly. They long for appreciation. On the other hand, they are extremely sensitive to criticisms and have a low tolerance when they are not gratified. People with the HPD resemble these traits as well.

Often, when histrionics and the people with HPD fail, they begin projecting their blame on others. This is actually a trait that is frequently observed in another personality disorder as well: the ***Narcissistic Personality Disorder***. But this does not come up as a surprise since histrionics and people with HPD share a good number of personality traits with narcissists. All these people enjoying blaming their personal failures on others.

The hedonism in histrionics and people with HPD results from their high intolerance to inactivity and routines. This also causes instability in both their personal and professional lives. In addition, this increases their risk-taking behavior.

For example, Apt C. and Hurlbert DF. (1994) suggest that women with HPD possess significantly greater sexual preoccupation than women with no HPD. Sexual preoccupation is referred to as hypersexuality or sexual addiction. It is a sexual practice that usually deviates from normative practice. The study emphasises that women with HPD tended to have lower sexual satisfaction with their partners and therefore, are more likely to engage in extramarital affairs than those women with no HPD.

For the same reason, people with HPD have instabilities in their professional lives as well. They struggle to find their true passion and doubt whether what they do makes them passionate. Thus, people with HPD change their jobs frequently, trying to endeavour on new adventures and experiences as they easily become bored.

I believe this level of understanding on histrionics is more than enough. As such, let's study how we can influence these people.

Influencing and Manipulating Histrionics

Throughout the chapter, you were presented with numerous information on histrionics that is intended to improve your relationships with them. Indeed, in an environment where you can build a rapport with someone and convert it into a meaningful relationship is the best way to remain influential in that person's life. As such, my first piece of advice would be to try and build a strong rapport with these people by adjusting your attitude based on everything that you have learned throughout this chapter. And know this; you have learned a lot.

But there are also instances where we basically do not have the leisure of building a strong rapport with someone. Indeed, this process is long and requires commitment, dedication and a lot of effort. There might be instances when we are short on time, or the situations may not allow to take things to a personal level. So, how do we get what we need from histrionics under such conditions?

For such cases, you were presented with several techniques of manipulation and influence. But there are also techniques that I did not teach. Let me go over them briefly below:

- ***No personal attacks***: Histrionics are sensitive and will not tolerate negative triggers.

- ***Credibility***: Do not use unless disproving them will gain you either a tangible or intangible payoff since by discrediting them, you will also be damaging any relationship with them permanently. Weigh pros and cons, i.e., if the payoffs from discrediting them exceed the loss of any chance in a respectful relationship.

- ***Be tactically sharp***: Be careful what you ask them. If you ask them difficult questions, it may end badly. To be specific, due to their superficial attitude, it is very likely that histrionics would not be able to answer either in a comprehensive, or in a detailed manner. If you received a response to your question and believe it lacks detail, do not surrender to the urge of asking a further question to clarify. Histrionics are not good with details. On the other hand, perform this if you intend to discredit them.

- ***Control your emotions***: Histrionics are provocative, tactless, and gauche. Thus, they can attempt a personal attack on you in order to provoke you. But always remain kind in such situations but do not bow on any occasion. Deliver your message to them in a way that they will understand and feel sorry about it. Silent treatment, contemptible laugh with a witty comeback, or ignore are among the right tools to employ. The probability of friendship is higher with such responses. Your task is to manifest a high status and strong inner power. It is most likely that histrionics will provoke you without being aware of it, so do not let them know that you are actually offended; otherwise, the situation might escalate.

- ***Keep your distance***: Be secretive and polite. Always protect your personal distance, though do not alienate them. Confide in them that you are indeed close to them, but you also have certain boundaries that they must respect. This is a golden rule when dealing with histrionics. Although histrionics are secretive for their friends, their relationships are very volatile since they are demanding. A mere offense may trigger them to rub anything they know about you on your face. In addition, do not give them what they want straight away.

- ***Approval***: This is a weak spot for histrionics. Ensure that you praise them once in a while, but also be careful not to get them used to it. Otherwise, they will begin taking it for granted and assume that they are indeed something exquisite. This technique is a healthy poison when used in smaller doses. The best way to use it is with empathy: understand what is bothering them, perhaps a problem they are having difficulty with. Then use your knowledge of their qualities and past experiences to praise them. For example, suppose a histrionic lady is whining about whether she could pursue a full-time job in the city. In that case, you may reply as: *"I have full* *confidence that not only you will get the job but will be promoted to a management position in a year or two. You are resourceful, creative and can think on your feet, and these are the important qualities listed on the job description"*. This approval works better if you can cite a few examples from their past where they showed that they were resourceful, creative, and able to think on their feet. Using this technique at proper times will go a long way in making the histrionic to confide her whole trust in you.

- *Annihilation*: Use it as a last resort since annihilating people is not a good thing to do. Employ it if it is necessary for saving your status or inflicting superiority.

- *Ignore*: Sometimes, taking attention away from a histrionic and directing it towards someone else will trigger him to try and earn that attention back. It is always better if you make them approach you. You may utilize the art of seduction to have people pursue you. If you are also physically appealing, witty, popular, well-dressed, and cool, then they are more likely to approach you without the need of seducing them.

- ***Seduction***: Remember the story of the Marquis de Sevigne and the young countess. The techniques of ***confusion, psychology of loss, jealousy, scarcity, social proof and element of surprise*** were used to seduce the young countess, which actually went quite perfectly until marquis could not help but blow it up.

Conclusion

Before we conclude, there is an interesting mnemonic developed by Harold Pinkofsky (1997) that is intended to make it easier for readers to remember the features of HPD. This mnemonic is known as *"PRAISE ME"*, each letter stands for one feature of the HPD. However, since all of these features are core characteristics of histrionic psychotype as well, feel free to use it:

P	Provocative (or sexually seductive) behavior
R	Relationships (considered more intimate than they are)
A	Attention (uncomfortable when not the center of attention)
I	Influenced easily
S	Style of speech (impressionistic, lacks detail)
E	Emotions (rapidly shifting and shallow)
M	Made up (physical appearance used to draw attention to self)
E	Emotions exagerrated (theatrical)

In this chapter, you have developed a very strong knowledge of histrionics, and I cannot wait for you to use these resources in practice. The following chart summarizes the key characteristics of the histrionic psychotype:

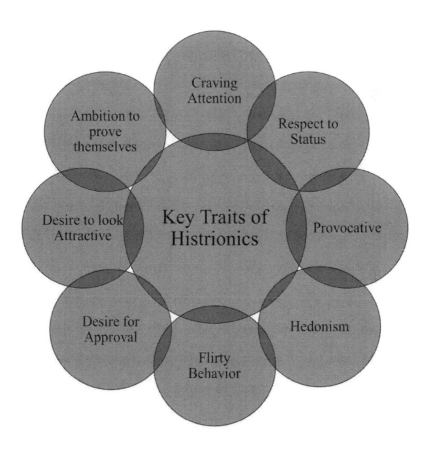

3

Epileptoids

"Anybody can become angry – that is easy, but to be angry with the right person and to the right degree and at the right time and for the right purpose, and in the right way – that is not within everybody's power and is not easy"

(Aristotle)

I started this chapter with a quote about anger management simply because we will study a psychotype whose members have issues managing their anger. These people are called "epileptoids". What is more, these people do not admit that they are angry – they blame people around them for making them angry. The reason why epileptoids have issues with rage is that they get overwhelmed by the ***accumulation of daily inflows of information, events, tasks, duties, and responsibilities***, which by overwhelming their nervous system, leads them to the state of explosion.

For example, wife asking to pick up the children, children being capricious, people asking too many questions, colleagues needing help, a friend being late for a meeting, several outstanding tasks that need to be completed in a short time frame, and so on. All these accumulate and cause affective explosions in epileptoids by overwhelming their mental state.

But why do epileptoids get overwhelmed when they can avoid these issues and not exhaust themselves with unnecessary things? The reason is that epileptoids cannot ignore anything. They want to have everything under control. They take every issue seriously in order to resolve it instantly. And it is common for them to worsen the situation with their strict approach because, by far, not every issue is a problem. As such, epileptoids overburden themselves.

Furthermore, since *epileptoids have a weak nervous system*, their mental capacity is naturally low. Hence, they cannot deal with huge inflows of external influences on their nervous system. Thus, they easily get overwhelmed, and once things they get overwhelmed with accumulate, they explode. The victims of such explosions are people near them at the time.

Before analyzing epileptoids, visualize a soldier in a military uniform and list down some of the character traits you believe he would have. I think your list would look something like this:

- Strict and serious
- Stiff and tough
- Resilient and hardworking
- Disciplined and organized
- Standard and monotonous thinking
- Tidy and neat
- Rule-follower and obedient

The best "hobby" of epileptoids is making rules and demanding others to follow them. This is because an environment that has a strict set of rules creates certainty and hence, reduces the amount of issues that an epileptoid will need to get himself involved with, i.e., "*everything is organized and will go according to the rules, right? I am probably not going to be bothered by anything in this case*".

When things do not progress according to rules, epileptoids get overwhelmed, which triggers irritation and explosion. For example, suppose your boss is an epileptoid and has given you a task with instructions on how to complete it. Assume you complete this task in a way that is more efficient but different to that of epileptoid's. How do you think your boss will react?

He will get irritated, even if your method is more efficient. This is because he will get overwhelmed. Think about it this way. The method your boss has instructed is the one that he is familiar with and is assured of its validity. Now, what you have done is to introduce a new method. Though it might be better, your boss does not know it, and trust me on this; epileptoids will never take your word for it. They are highly cautious and sceptical. Your boss will need to go through every step of your method, analyze it, and then conclude whether it is suitable. As you can see, these are the new flows of information that need to be dealt with. Hence, you will further exhaust an already overwhelmed state of mind, hence, trigger irritation.

Epileptoids are responsible, disciplined and organized. They have clear schedules and timetables, as they always want things to go according to a plan. As such, they possess a systematic and structural attitude. They pay extensive attention to accuracy, tidiness and cleanness. The reason behind all these is obvious. **Such practices reduce the exhaustion of epileptoids.**

Think of it this way. Will it be easier for you to find a pair of socks to wear in the morning if they lay neatly in your wardrobe or if they have declared their independence and are rooming messily around the house? I think the answer is clear. That is why epileptoids possess such personality traits. These practices make their life easier. When the many channels and inflows of information, data, events and activities are managed in a systematic, accurate, and structured manner, they can be handled easily without a reason to get exhausted or overwhelmed.

Now, having learned these, can you guess the fundamental character trait of epileptoids? For histrionics, it was the concept of "self-importance". What do you think is the fundamental trait of epileptoids, given the aforementioned personality traits?

It is their desire to *live a predictable life and maintain their safety*. This is what drives epileptoid's mental state and his actions. Desire for predictability, safety, and stability are the fundamental character traits of epileptoid.

For this reason, epileptoids do not ignore anything and get themselves involved in every possible issue that concerns them even slightly. As a result, they get overwhelmed, and consequently, they have no other choice but to explode.

Why do we call these people as *"epileptoids"*. This comes from the mental condition called *"epilepsy"*. Epilepsy is a disorder when the electrical activity in the brain increases so much that it begins to burst suddenly, which causes seizures. Similarly, epileptoids get themselves involved in so many issues that they consequently get overwhelmed, and then, they explode.

Now, since epileptoids love certainty and stability in their lives, they maintain a monotonous lifestyle while simultaneously avoiding novelty and facing difficulties when accustoming to changes. This is called *"inertia"* – the tendency to remain unchanged or to do nothing new.

This personality trait of epileptoids might start showing itself later in adulthood or in early adolescence. It depends when an epileptoid reaches his comfort zone. Once the epileptoid feels totally comfortable in his current state of life, the traits of inertia start appearing visibly. Epileptoids naturally possess inertia as they do not want to overwhelm themselves with new things.

Inertia

Inertia is defined as the tendency to remain unchanged or to do nothing new. The reason why epileptoids have inertia is that they love stability and certainty in their lives.

This feature of epileptoids affects their entire psyche, from motor and emotionality all the way to their thought process and personal values. The inertia of epileptoids can be observed in their:

- ***Social activities***: They do not like unexpected activities. Assume an epileptoid is seated and is watching television. Suddenly, his wife asks him to go to the cinema. How do you think an epileptoid will react? Well, the answer will definitely be no. It is hard to pull epileptoids from their seats. Also, they do not like facilitating social activities so do not get your hopes up with epileptoids.

- ***Thought process***: They have a standard thought process that they apply to every situation. Sometimes, such an approach may be inefficient or irrelevant given the context or nature of the problem. Nonetheless, they don't like approaching problems in a creative manner as they do not want to bother and overwhelm themselves.

- ***Personal values***: These people tend to be stubborn with their values, morals, beliefs, and worldview. Once they have established a certain belief system, it is very difficult to change it. For that reason, they are very obstinate.

Inertia is almost always observed in their social and personal lives. But the determining factor of whether an epileptoid has the inertia in his professional life will depend on him reaching his *"comfort zone"*. For example, an epileptoid looking for a job will be very hardworking to get the position he wants. Until he reaches his goal, he will be very persistent. This comes from the **demand for having a stable life in the long run**.

Nonetheless, once they reach their aims and goals, inertia starts showing itself. But do not get confused. An epileptoid will still remain working productively and effectively since he wants to keep his job in the long-term. The way it will show itself is in lack or declined level of ambition.

Assume that an epileptoid gentleman has reached his comfort zone, e.g., he has a full-time job and earns a salary that he finds adequate for him and his family. Also, assume that he works from 09:00 to 17:00. At 17:00, he will want to come straight to home – the place where he can relax and where he feels comfortable. After having his dinner, he will engage in an activity that does not take too much energy or effort; simply, something that does not overwhelm him. Most often, this involves watching TV. Then he will go to sleep and wake up the next day to go to work at 9 am in the morning.

This will be his lifestyle until retirement: the same workplace, the same area of work, and the same routine. What is more, he will probably stop looking for any job opportunities that might promise higher salaries or career opportunities simply because he would not want to overwhelm himself. He cannot bother with all the recruitment process, adapting to a new working environment, getting to know new people and so on. All these are troubling thoughts for epileptoids.

For this reason, histrionics or hyperthymics suffer a great deal when they are married to epileptoids. Rarely, it is possible to get an epileptoid to go out, but he must be back at home no later than 10 pm. For that reason, if you are married to an epileptoid, then kiss goodbye to your late-night activities.

Now that we have finished studying the inertia of epileptoids, we can move on to our next subject – the thought process of epileptoids. These people have a gradual and weak nervous system. The fundamental idea is that they want everything around them to be under their control. This is due to, of course, their desire for certainty and stability. They feel much safer and comfortable when things happening around are under their control.

Uncertainty causes *anxiety* in epileptoids. On the other hand, maintaining control is a challenging endeavour. It is simply *overwhelming.* Once epileptoids get overwhelmed, the state of *anger and dysphoria begins*, which then leads to *explosions.*

Thought Process

Epileptoids want to control the large flows of information and events. And they try not to forget anything. However, once these flows of information and events accumulate, it starts to pose huge pressure on epileptoid's mind. Of course, this would pose immense mental pressure on anyone, but most people endure this without exploding. The reason why epileptoids are the ones to explode in these situations is because of two reasons:

1) They overwhelm themselves even with issues that are not really important. This is because they do not ignore anything since they fear it could affect them negatively.

2) They have a weak nervous system; therefore, they do not have enough capacity to deal with large flows of new developments, information, events, and activities.

Now, to strengthen our understanding of this, let us ask ourselves two questions. Firstly, some psychotypes also have a weak nervous system, such as emotives and histrionics, but exploding is not commonly observed in their nature. Why? Because the members of these psychotypes do not bother themselves with every issue around them – they simply do not exhaust themselves purposefully as epileptoids do. However, for epileptoids, getting overwhelmed, even with the slightest issues, is almost a daily routine.

Another question that you can ask yourself is why members of other psychotypes, the fanatic psychotype in particular, who also get themselves immensely overwhelmed by trying to control all and everything happening around, do not explode? The reason is straightforward. Fanatics have a strong nervous system, unlike epileptoids. The behavior of getting themselves overwhelmed is identical between fanatics and epileptoids. However, fanatics, by having a strong nervous system, are extremely resilient to getting overwhelmed, and they can deal with it naturally. But epileptoids have a weak nervous system. Hence, they explode after some point.

It is common for epileptoids to get exhausted, and thus, it is common for them to explode. Here we get to an interesting point – an existential dilemma let us say for epileptoids. On the one hand, epileptoids have a weak nervous system, hence, they should basically stop worrying and trying to deal with every single thing. This would lift the immense burden that they assign on themselves.

But on the other hand, they cannot do it since they want to live a predictable life and maintain their safety. Hence, they involve themselves in everything and try to fix every problem. In some cases, they worsen the situation since not every issue is a problem. By biting more than they can chew, epileptoids lead themselves to an explosive state. Living a simpler, easier and stress-free life is not for epileptoids. They "must" get stressed.

When studying their external appearance, you will learn that epileptoids have a muscular body type due to keeping their muscles constantly under stress.

Epileptoids have a ***gradual nervous system***, which implies that their reactions to things in life are neither instantaneous nor late. That is, they take enough time to think and process information before responding. For this reason, people with a gradual nervous system are ***analytical***.

Epileptoids are also ***detail-oriented*** because if any detail is missed, the conclusion would not be accurate. This idea is frustrating for epileptoids because if an important detail is disregarded, then there is a likelihood that the control over the situation could go away. This raises uncertainty, which frustrates epileptoids. As such, if they think they have missed a detail, they will get stuck and try to remember it.

Epileptoids try to remember all the details so that they can proceed without getting anxious or frustrated. This, in turn, leads to a stronger memory because epileptoids constantly train their memory by recalling all the details, without even noticing it! This, of course, comes with a price. Epileptoids will get themselves involved in more-than-necessary details and put an unnecessary burden on their mental state.

Since it leads to an explosion, epileptoids fear getting overwhelmed. What mechanisms do you think epileptoids develop to avoid this? If you linked the answer to being structural, systematic, organized, tidy, and neat, then you are right.

To avoid getting overwhelmed with too many things, and to process them efficiently, epileptoids develop a systematic and structural attitude. Epileptoids plan their work well ahead by keeping organized timetables and schedules. Planning plays an integral part in their life since it avoids forgetting important things that need to be done.

I have always witnessed that epileptoids have a very organised outlook, google, or other forms of online calendars. Mostly, epileptoids plan their day a night ahead. Some even draft a timetable for the entire week on Saturdays or Sundays. This helps them visualize what targets need to be achieved in a structured manner. And they cope with it perfectly. After hypothymics, epileptoids are the ones who fulfil their responsibilities in the most efficient way.

If epileptoids get to deviate from their plains, they quickly get *irritated* since it overwhelms them. Why? Well, a schedule is like a house of cards: pull one away and the rest will come crashing down. Epileptoids understand this perfectly. They know that if they deviate from one of their plans, then they will need to rearrange the rest of their responsibilities. For this reason, epileptoids are very punctual.

Assume an epileptoid has a meeting with you. Unless something delays him, he will be there on time. He will also expect you to arrive on time. In case you are running late, he will start getting irritated and such thoughts will develop in his mind:

- My time is important; he has no right to keep me waiting

- He must have a reasonable explanation on why he is late

- I have rescheduled my timetable to meet him and look at the "respect" I am getting in return

- If he does not come in 5 minutes, I am shooting off

Of course, none of us would like to be kept waiting, but this affects epileptoids more than other psychotypes. Compared to other psychotypes, epileptoids have the least tolerance to unpunctuality. As you can see from the inner dialogue of the epileptoid above, there is an increasing tension in his mind as he is being kept waiting. But this tension will start declining the moment he sees that you have arrived and that you are making your way towards him.

But he will wait for you to apologise and provide a fair reason. An apology alone will not be enough; he will want to hear that he has been kept waiting for a good cause. If you provide a reasonable excuse, then he will relax completely. Otherwise, he will be very judgemental towards you. The best thing to do, of course, is to notify them that you will be running late in advance.

Pragmatism and present-time oriented perspective: We have put enough thought into how epileptoids love to have things under control due to their love of stability. We also learned how they get overwhelmed from trying to control everything around, and what kind of traits they develop to cope with it. Now, we will learn how epileptoid's need for predictability makes them pragmatic and present-time oriented, and then move on to studying their analytical skills.

Present time-oriented perspective: Epileptoids set up their life based on *"now and here"*. For example, if you offer an epileptoid a business opportunity, he will ask you about short-term earnings. If most of the returns will be realized in the distant future (say 5 – 10 years), he will not be satisfied with it. Due to being present time-oriented (due to their dislike of uncertainty), epileptoids are more focused on the immediate concrete factors with little regard to possible factors that may happen in the future.

This is another reason (apart from inertia) why epileptoids do not embark on new opportunities. Because the evaluation of success is based on the future factors, epileptoids do not like. For example, if you offer your epileptoid friend to leave his job to run a start-up with you, he will probably say no. But if you set up the company first and then offer him an employment position, he will be more likely to accept. As such, epileptoids are not the best entrepreneurs and innovators. In fact, there is no epileptoid entrepreneur that I am familiar with. Having worked in finance, I have met many, though none was an epileptoid.

Pragmatism: Epileptoids are inclined towards acting rather than theorizing. They tend to be overly pragmatic. Unlike schizoids, who prefer to theorize and dream about a given task, epileptoids want to perform it. However, when a task is given to an epileptoid, it needs to be structured, and the information should be complete. Otherwise, epileptoid will perform the task in a way that will not lead to the desired outcome, only because the task was not delegated to him in an accurate and structured way.

Also, they may do a completely different task only because they did not understand the information. This is a character trait of schizoids, i.e., when you give a task to a schizoid, he will most likely do something different instead.

Epileptoids, in this sense, are the complete opposites of schizoids. Schizoids are frequently called *"dreamers"* because they have rich fantasy world and love to come up with new creative ideas. Unlike them, epileptoids hate dreams; they prefer to live in reality. For this reason, it is almost impossible to find an inventor, innovator, or an academic among epileptoids.

Analytical Skills

We have already mentioned how epileptoids process information in a structured way. They like to break down the information into several pieces first. Afterward, they consider every piece of information in detail in order to get the results. Epileptoids have strong attention to detail and strong analytical skills.

Analytical skill is the ability to break down the information into smaller parts (called 'deconstruction') to draw conclusions. Having strong analytical skills involves having strong:

- Observational skills

- Critical thinking skills

- Logical reasoning skills: includes deductive, inductive, and abductive reasoning skills

Epileptoids only have *strong deductive-reasoning, critical thinking, and observational skills*. They usually do not apply inductive or abductive reasoning as the conclusions drawn may not always be true or applicable. Such skills are more suitable in the areas requiring creativity, such as academic research. Remember, these are the areas that epileptoids do not get involved in. As such, let's keep these aside, though you might find it interesting to read about these on your own time.

Now, deductive reasoning starts with having a few pieces of information or statements together and then drawing a conclusion from these statements. For example, assume you have two statements:

1) People with a fast nervous system have a superficial attitude

2) Histrionics and hyperthymics have a fast nervous system

We can conclude from these two statements that histrionics and hyperthymics have a superficial attitude. This is called deductive reasoning. However, all of your statements must be true for deductive reasoning to work. Consider this, for example:

1) People with a fast nervous system have a natural eye for detail

2) Histrionics and hyperthymics have a fast nervous system

We can conclude from these two statements that histrionics and hyperthymics have an eye for detail. But this is not true because neither histrionics nor hyperthymics are detail-oriented. Although the process of deductive reasoning is valid, the conclusion drawn is incorrect since the first statement is wrong.

Therefore, deductive-reasoning works if it is accompanied by strong observational and critical thinking skills. Let me explain. In real life, valid statements do not grow on trees. We need to find these ourselves. With the help of strong observational skills, we may be able to gather data and information, which we can later clean and form statements. Once we have enough statements, we will have to check their validity. For this, we will need strong critical thinking skills since it is all about analyzing facts, statements, and other forms of information in order to form judgments.

Once you have formed judgements on each piece of information, you now have statements on which you can apply your deductive reasoning skills. Such an approach guarantees that deductive reasoning is applied to both *relevant* and *valid* pieces of information:

- Relevant because due to strong observational skills, you have gathered only the relevant information.

- Valid because due to strong critical thinking skills, you have validated the true statements and dismissed the false ones.

Having talked about deductive reasoning, let us move on to *critical thinking*, which we have already mentioned above. It is the evaluation of any form information, such as quantitative or qualitative, in order to form an opinion. Having strong critical thinking skill requires one to be *rational, sceptical, and unbiased* when it comes to information that is not factual evidence. Because epileptoids are naturally sceptical and rational, they tend to excel in critical thinking.

Last but not the least, epileptoids are very observational people. Let me give a personal example on how observational epileptoids can be. My father is an epileptoid. Once we were walking on the sidewalk. We had bungalows on the right, and on the left, we had the highway. He felt silent and started paying attention to the altitude of the sidewalk and the road. He then started telling me:

"Salim, you see that the altitude of the road is above the altitude of the sideway. However, it should be the other way around so that when it rains, the water from the sideway can flow into the road, and from there, into the drainage so that there is no water accumulated in front of these properties. This implies that bungalows were built before the highway. Because if the highway was built first, then architectures of these bungalows would have adjusted the altitude to be above the road".

From this example, can you see how observational epileptoids are? Who walks on the sideway and observes such details? Let alone observe, we usually walk on the streets without even turning our face from left to right. Also, look at how strong was his deductive-reasoning: from the highway's altitude being above the sideways, he deduced that the highway was built after the bungalows. I got interested if this was the case. In fact, when the bungalows were built there in the 1960s, that road was merely a rural route. However, due to the region's expansion of population, the road was reconstructed into a highway in 2012.

Overall, epileptoids are very observational people. I understand that explaining character traits of psychotypes only in a written way may not be the best approach. As such, I always give references from the real life or from movies and series. As such, I would suggest you to watch one of the Netflix Original Series: "Lilyhammer". The main character, "Giovanni Henriksen", is a member of epileptoid psychotype.

Dysphoria and Explosiveness

One of the most prominent character traits of epileptoids is the ***propensity to dysphoria***. Dysphoria is defined as the general state of unhappiness, restlessness, dissatisfaction, or frustration.

Why do you think epileptoids have a tendency to dysphoria? The fundamental reason is that ***they want to control everything***. However, this is where the dysphoria begins. As you have studied in the previous section, such behavior of epileptoids gets them overwhelmed as they have a weak nervous system. An overwhelmed state of mind leads to a state of explosion. As such, the reason why epileptoids get into dysphoric states is due to two reasons:

1) The desire for everything to go according to plan and to be under their control

2) Lack of mental capacity due to the weak nervous system

The general state of dysphoria makes epileptoids more introverted than extroverted. Although they do not get overwhelmed by social interactions the way schizoids or hypothymics do, epileptoids often prefer being alone. Dysphoria may last for hours or even days. It is built when they get overwhelmed by excessive tasks, increased responsibilities, a new environment, negative life events, such as sickness in an immediate family member, and so on. Dysphoria of epileptoids is noticeable by their radiant irritation and sometimes, their search for an object on which to unleash the evil (something to hit or kick).

Because dysphoria visits epileptoids frequently, the self-aware ones tend to isolate themselves in calmer environments since they are aware that they will explode at someone. Thus, they want to avoid it. The calmer the environment, the easier it is for dysphoria to dissipate, and during complete solitude, epileptoids reach tranquillity.

The *affective explosions* of epileptoids are caused by dysphoria. These seem sudden at first glance, but these explosions actually resemble a steam boiler, which boils gradually at first, but after some time, explodes. That is, epileptoid's explosion is the accumulation of instances when he got overwhelmed. Every time when gets overwhelmed, he tries to keep his cool; he decides not to lose it, not to explode. But after some time, these feelings accumulate, he tries to find a calmer environment – to isolate himself from everyone around him. If he fails, then after a few moments, he will completely lose his self-control. Hence, he will explode. The cause of such an explosion can be completely random, triggered by the last drop.

So, the affective explosions of epileptoids happen when they are at dysphoric state. Also, these explosions are usually triggered by the last drop. The person triggering it is not to fully blame for the rage and anger of the epileptoid. Remember the quote by Aristotle at the beginning of this chapter:

"Anybody can become angry – that is easy, but to be angry with the right person and to the right degree and at the right time and for the right purpose, and in the right way – that is not within everybody's power and is not easy"

If an epileptoid explodes at you, then know that you are not to fully blame; you just played your role as the *"last drop"*. It falls to their fault that they are not angry with the right person, to the right degree and for the right purpose, and in the right way. As if Aristotle left this quote for epileptoids to read and tame themselves. Epileptoids usually explode when they experience high levels of dysphoria, and in these moments, even the slightest conflict can lead them to burst out.

The explosions of epileptoids are frequently caused by the last drop. These most frequently happen in the form of social conflicts. Social conflicts are quite common in epileptoids' lives because of their stubborn, dissatisfied and demanding nature. The last drop – the reason for anger – might be small or even insignificant, but it always entails at least a minor infringement of interests. The vegetative accompaniment of affective explosions is also observed in epileptoids – their face gets filled with blood, sweat, and so on.

But it is also frequent to observe epileptoids seeking a cause for scandal when they are at somewhat dysphoric state, even when there is no one causing any conflict. In other words, epileptoids are looking for a reason to explode. I call this an ***attempt for affective discharges***.

Sometimes, epileptoids get so overwhelmed that they feel a huge level of discomfort. Assume that epileptoid endures dysphoria, and given the circumstances, he cannot isolate himself. Also, assume that there is no one around overwhelming him – no one pours the last drop. In this case, he will walk around anxiously and try to find some victim to explode at. This is because the only way he will be able to escape dysphoria is to discharge.

Basically, epileptoid wants to explode and discharge himself in order to be able to start feeling better again. Therefore, if you see that an epileptoid is picking fights with people during a day, where people characterize such behavior as *"got up on the wrong side of the bed"*, then understand that he needs to discharge. It is better to avoid them in such moments so that you are not the one who endures the explosion of the epileptoid, unless you want to do a public service, of course.

Among all people, hyperthymics, histrionics and epileptoids tend to excel at sports. But I would say that epileptoids are the most successful in this area because sports help them to discharge. Most epileptoids prefer engaging in martial art, such as boxing. Such areas of sport allow to discharge the negative energy and reach tranquillity. Therefore, if you have an epileptoid wife or husband, find a way to engage in some physical activities – it will hugely reduce the stress on your relationship.

The explosive state of epileptoids differs not only by the magnitude of rage but also by its duration, i.e., epileptoids cannot cool down for a long time. As such, these explosions differ from the easily occurring and rapidly depleting explosions of histrionics and hyperthymics. To be specific, epileptoids' explosive state differs from the short-tempered explosive state of hyperthymics and histrionics, who burst out easily but just as easily cool down. This is because of their shallowness caused by their fast nervous system.

When does dysphoria begin to appear in epileptoids? Well, it starts at teenage years. These states of dysphoria occur spontaneously so that even epileptoid teenagers cannot explain its origins. The dysphoria manifests itself in either being capricious or with a wave of moody anger. They also have a strong sense of ownership that pursues them to adulthood. This is usually observed in the frugality of their clothes, toys, and everything that belongs to them. Any attempts to "attack" the properties of epileptoids are met with negative reactions.

I would not give this as a general example for epileptoids, but I would like you to remember the character "Mountain" from the "Game of Thrones" series. He was a psychopathic epileptoid. Recall that when seeing his little brother, later known as the "Hound", playing with his toy, he got so raged that he burnt his brother's face. This is because epileptoids get frustrated when seeing their belongings in the hands of others – they are worried about the fate of their possessions. But only a psychopath would not be able to handle a light frustration and end up burning his brother's face for it.

Epileptoids never forget or forgive the harm caused to them. As such, they tend to be vindictive. In the cases of extreme accentuation, they would get pleasure from observing the pain they have delivered to their offenders. But this will be the case only when the accentuation of character is at the level of pathology, or if an epileptoid has mental or behavioral disorder, such as the antisocial personality disorder.

I would like to give a real-life example for this, which is quite entertaining. This case was observed by Lichko (1982). A 14-year-old epileptoid teenager had a mother who had divorced his father. For this reason, he assumed the role of a supreme – the man of the house. But later, his mother married someone, and his reign came to an end. For this reason, he hated his stepfather and did something that blew my mind when I read about it. He rubbed the inner surface of his stepfather's condoms with spicy caustic pepper. Later, he enjoyed listening to his stepfather's cries from his bedroom.

Please do not allow these two examples to bias you against epileptoids. In both cases, we had epileptoids at pathological states of mind. I want to state that most people in my life with whom I am close are members of the epileptoid psychotype. Both my parents are genetic epileptoids. Do you think that I suffered the severe negative traits of their character? Not at all.

Epileptoids who have strong morals, conscience, dignity, self-respect, and respect for others are extremely truthful and honest and would sacrifice their comfort for their family and friends. As long as they do not suffer from any mental disorders, there is nothing terrible about their character (though their fury and explosions are subject to debate).

I would like to give a fictional example for epileptoids so that you do not form severe opinions on epileptoids. Hopefully, you've watched the "Harry Potter". In this film, the character "Professor Minerva McGonagall" is a typical epileptoid:

Behavior and External Appearance

Epileptoids have a stiff emotional state. Their mimicry and gestures are rigid and stable. Unlike histrionics, their mood does not experience rapid shifts. They look cold-blooded as they do not show their emotions because of their cautious and sceptical attitude. They are worried that people might take advantage of them if they show their soft side. They seek to maintain their safety, and they regard expressing emotions as expressing weakness.

For this reason, when you go out for drinks with epileptoids, once they get tipsy or drunk, they will become extremely friendly – you will see the emotional and friendly part of them that they rarely show in their daily lives. However, the feeling of embarrassment and uneasiness is likely to dominate epileptoids the next morning when they recall the night.

Due to the constant stress that epileptoids endure, they frequently keep their muscles under pressure. You can easily notice this from their handshakes. Epileptoids have firm and stiff handshakes. If a histrionic pays attention to gentle gestures while communicating, epileptoids use intense gestures. Although they give impressions dooming them as aggressive, it is their unique behaving style.

Research on the external appearance of epileptoids is extensive. If I am not wrong, it was Grunya Sukhareva (1959) who, for the first time, discovered and put forward the external and physical appearance of epileptoids:

- Strong physical development

- Massive torso

- Short but firm limbs

- A round head slightly pressed into the shoulders

- Big lower jaw

- Large genitals in males (take Grunya's word for it, I have not checked personally)

- Slow movements

- Heavy motor skills (i.e., heavily standing, walking, running, and so on)

Among all people, epileptoids are the ones who stun others by creating an impression of a reliable person. This is because they are highly responsible, and it is visible to others. Of course, a person who is extremely punctual, cares about his safety, is disciplined and organized, tidy and neat, systematic and accurate, and pays attention to details is a dictionary definition of *"responsible"*. For this reason, people put immense trust in them. People usually have the opinion of *"man of his word"* about epileptoids.

Social Relationships

Now, since epileptoids explode once they get overwhelmed, they start fearing it since it ruins their social image and personal relationships with people. For the reason that epileptoids may get overwhelmed in social environments, they prefer communicating with people who maintain a structured and mutual dialogue. When they hear information from someone, they want it to be presented in steps. This helps to manage overwhelming information in a structured way without exploding.

If they do not understand the beginning of the conversation, they hardly follow because they get anxious. Furthermore, people need to keep a normal pace of conversation with epileptoids. Epileptoids cannot stop analyzing information, hence, if too much information is thrown at them at a short period of time, they will get overwhelmed, and this will trigger anxiety, which could then lead to dysphoria.

Epileptoids are highly sceptical – a feature that develops due to their urge for safety. Such scepticism is observed even in their relationships with family members and close friends. Epileptoids are very careful in choosing their friends. If these people call you a friend, they will never betray you. However, people often dislike the "scepticism" of epileptoids since they are distrustful and almost always push others to prove their loyalty.

For example, if you tell your mother about your new boyfriend, and assuming that your mother is an epileptoid, then she will start asking too many questions about your new boyfriend. These questions will be in the form of "*how do you know you can trust this guy?*". As such, epileptoids channel their exhaustion to others.

Epileptoids have a strong sense of righteousness about how things should be done. That is, they are the only ones who know how to do something right, while others do not. As such, epileptoids do not like being questioned on their capabilities. They are also very stubborn. They would rather continue arguing with you than consider the possibility that they might be wrong.

However, they do not tolerate people who do not admit to being wrong. They are somewhat hypocritical in this sense. If they are wrong, then they will exhaust you completely until you convince them that your point is right. But if you are wrong, then they will get irritated and might even explode if you do not agree with them instantaneously.

Epileptoids have a nasty habit when presenting them with new information. For example, assume that your friend is an epileptoid and he works in the field of criminal law. If you mention a term in criminal law that he has not heard about, he will immediately tell you that you are wrong. This is a character trait that all epileptoids should try to avoid. Just because you have not read or heard of something, it does not mean that it does not exist. But the strong sense of righteousness of epileptoids causes them to act as such, i.e., *"if I do not know this, then either it does not exist, or it is wrong"*.

Epileptoids get themselves involved in every possible issue that concerns them even slightly. When this happens in social environments, e.g., when an epileptoid gets involved in his colleague's problems in the workplace and tries to solve them for him, this may create a wrong social perception. Situations like these may lead others to think that epileptoids have a saviour complex. That is not the case. Though it is true that people with "saviour complex" spend a lot of time and energy trying to fix issues of others, and consequently, they end up "burning out", it is not the case for epileptoids. Epileptoids do not spend any energy on trying to fix things that are not any of their concern.

Let us think about this logically. These people already have a low level of mental energy due to constantly being overwhelmed. As such, will they further exhaust themselves by trying to solve issues that are not of any concern to them? Of course not!

For example, if an epileptoid's colleague in a workplace is feeling down, epileptoid will not approach to talk to him. He will say that it is his personal issue, and he can deal with it on his own time, as long as it does not interfere with the job. On the other hand, if his colleague has a task that he cannot complete, and this would affect epileptoid's performance as well, then he will interfere and try to solve the task for his colleague. But he will do it with great displeasure and will repeatedly label his colleague as incompetent or irresponsible. So, as long as issues of other people do not affect epileptoids, they will not interfere.

In the workplace, epileptoids aim to fulfil only their own responsibilities, unless someone asks them for help. In this situation, epileptoid will help but in his own way. The work will have to be done according to the epileptoid's approach, and if his colleague disagrees with him at any point, epileptoid will become irritated. He will likely respond, "*okay, from now on, do it yourself the way you see fit*".

As you can see from here, epileptoids like control. If you ask their help with something, they will take the complete ownership of that task until they deliver it to you. If at any moment you interfere and try to manage them while they are working on it, they will become angry and ask you to either step aside or do the task on your own.

Now, I would like to make a very important point. When you interact with others, some people will respond to you based on what you have said or how you have said it. I call this behavior as ***"relevant reactions"***. For example, if your friend is an emotive, the more friendly you get, the friendlier she will get with you. But there are also other people who might react towards you in a completely irrelevant manner regardless of your actions. I call this as ***"irrelevant reactions"***.

Schizoids are classic examples who belong to the class of people with irrelevant reactions. For example, if you give a task to schizoid, e.g., call it ABC, then most likely he will deliver something different, e.g., say XYZ. When I worked with children at primary schools, I have always heard from the teachers that some students always deliver a completely different thing instead of the original homework. If the homework is to write about the importance of family bonds, these students write about the importance of friendships or anything they want to write about. All these students were the members of schizoid psychotype.

Epileptoids, on the other hand, belong to a class of people with *"relevant reactions"*. Unlike schizoids, epileptoids interpret the signals based on the environment and the context. For example, they analyze people's behavior in order to come to conclusions.

Unlike them, schizoids do not care, and they do not analyze their social surroundings. This is because they get lost in their thought. For instance, before making a joke, epileptoids think about whether the environment is appropriate for jokes. However, schizoids would not care about this. If they want to crack a joke, they will go ahead and do it, even if cracking a joke is completely inappropriate given the environment that they are in.

Epileptoids

Schizoids can start singing all of a sudden while walking on the street or start laughing at a memory that has crossed their minds. Before doing so, they will not think whether others will interpret it as weird or inappropriate. Schizoids cannot feel those around them because they lack intuition. For example, a schizoid can pass by his friend without even greeting him, but epileptoids take it seriously to greet and to be greeted by people, especially by their friends.

Since epileptoids belong to people with relevant reactions, the first impression is very important for them. Unlike histrionics, they are not so vulnerable to the *"halo effect"*. That is, they are not inclined as much towards formulating either positive or negative opinions on one's personality based on their external appearance. But they do pay attention whether a person is dressed appropriately. They also pay close attention to one's voice tone, topics he talks about, and his social behavior.

Epileptoids are not a fan of those who speak loudly, as they associate it with exhibitionist and superficial behavior, which they do not like. Also, they do not like those who have a fast-paced speech. This is because epileptoids pay close attention to details, and additionally, they are naturally very sceptical. If one speaks very quickly, then he is not giving enough time to epileptoid to process the information. In these situations, epileptoids get either overwhelmed or suspicious, e.g., *"he is moving from one topic to another maybe because he is not telling the truth"*.

Epileptoids love observing people. They look closely at the behaviors of people around them. Unsurprisingly, they divide people into two groups: ones who are worthy of talking to and others who should be ignored. For this reason, do not strive to get the attention of an epileptoid by doing something extraordinary because regardless, they will be observing you. It is a better strategy to act thoughtfully, responsibly, considerately, and friendly with those around you. In this case, epileptoid will start developing positive feelings towards you and will likely approach you. There will be a massive opportunity for friendship as well. It is even better to do so since they will feel safer around you. Never forget, safety is the utmost desire of epileptoids.

Lack of Appreciation

The most important thing you need to keep in mind when formulating relationships with epileptoids is that they are highly negative people because of the state of dysphoria they are constantly in. Some epileptoids spend most of their lives under the dysphoric state without even noticing it. They just get used to it. For this reason, epileptoids almost always exhibit negative and unsatisfied emotions.

Since epileptoids frequently think about things that could go wrong, they channel it on their social relationships as well. For instance, they cannot praise people at all. Let us assume that your father is an epileptoid. Now, if you are someone who constantly achieves high grades in school, then his reaction would be: "*this is your responsibility to succeed in school. Why should I praise you for doing your job?*". That is, epileptoids take the successful things that people do for granted. But if you get a below-than-average grade in one of your classes, then your father will immediately notice it, bring it to your attention and condemn you for it. Even if it was the first time you got a bad grade.

For example, suppose you are an epileptoid's employee, and let us assume that you constantly deliver your responsibilities successfully. Indeed, you will receive somewhere close to zero appreciation from your boss. But in case you fail once, even something so insignificant that does not have a measurable impact on the job, then your boss will immediately flashlight your failure and start condemning you for it, saying things like: "*You see!*

You mess up as usual!". Here the keyword is *"as usual"*. What the hell does he mean *"as usual"*? You have always delivered your responsibilities, but your boss labels you as someone who constantly messes up in the first instance of your slightest failure.

So, it is very rare and even impossible for epileptoids to praise people. For example, saying things like "*well done, great job, keep doing what you are doing*" is nearly unbearable for epileptoids. That is why they are not good at motivating people. But in case you fail for the first time, then the situation must be immediately escalated, and you must be condemned for it very badly.

Now, how can you avoid this? That is, how can you ensure that an epileptoid in your life does not take things you do for granted or does not condemn you when you fail? First of all, never give the ***illusion of control*** to epileptoids. That is to say, never allow epileptoids to think that they are in charge. Epileptoids respect authority, and as long as you resemble it, they would not attempt taking your work for granted or condemning you when you fail, simply because they ***would not have any standing in the situation***. But epileptoids naturally thrive on being in charge. So, is it possible to prevent them from thinking that they are in charge?

To begin with, always *keep a distance* with epileptoids. Never let them too close to your personal life and never show your weaknesses to them. Assume that your father is an epileptoid. Let's say that you are having a conflict with a friend. So, you approach him to ask for his guidance. This is a bad idea. Because even though he might help you, there is a good chance that he will use this against you in the future when it is the two of you that are having a conflict. At that moment, he will remind you of your past conflict with your friend and label you as someone who always ends up in disputes with people.

This is one of the manipulation techniques that I call *"character evidence"*. When I developed it as a manipulation technique, I named it as such since I had the idea from the actual law practice:

> *"character evidence is evidence used in the court of law in order to prove that a person has acted in a certain way on a certain occasion due to his personality or temperament"*

This technique can be used manipulatively by reminding someone of a certain situation that they were involved in the past, which is similar to the situation they are in today, with the sole purpose of using it against them. In our example, when you have ended up in a conflict with your father, he reminded you of your past conflict with a friend, labelling you as someone ending in conflicts with everyone around him. Even though you could have been in the right and your friend in the wrong, your father would not refrain from using it against you. Even if he agrees that you were right in that moment.

Another advantage of maintaining distance with epileptoids is in *gaining their respect*. Epileptoids respect discreet people and view them as strong. They have a natural tendency to respect and find comfort in those people who are careful and secretive, since these are some of the most important character traits that epileptoids have. As long as you maintain distance from them, they will respect you, and in this situation, they will not attempt to condemn you.

Another way to influence epileptoids, apart from maintaining a distance from them, is to **never allow them to burden you with responsibilities**. In fact, when epileptoids ask you to do something, think twice or thrice before accepting it. Do not promise anything you would not be able to deliver. Also, try not to agree to anything that is not any of your concern. But if you have made a promise, then ensure to deliver it.

Know this: epileptoids are hardworking and take ownership of their tasks. But they also strictly demand it from others. If you fail and make an excuse, then epileptoid will get angry simply because he will get overwhelmed by your excuses. Keep in mind, epileptoids are almost always overwhelmed and you throwing extra excuses at them might achieve nothing but act as the last drop leading them to the state of explosion. What you should do on such occasions, i.e., when you failed to deliver your responsibility, is to quickly tell the epileptoid about it, admit your guilt, and then pray to god for some mercy.

Furthermore, epileptoids cannot abide those who would not own up to their mistakes. If you ask me, from which psychotypes epileptoids get overwhelmed the most, my answer would be histrionics and hyperthymics. Because of their superficial and careless attitude, members of these psychotypes rarely admit their guilt; hence, epileptoids get overwhelmed from them frequently.

Similarly, ***do not do any favours to epileptoids***. Since they almost always take things for granted, they will downgrade any favor you have done for them. But if you have something that could help them, then wait until they ask for it. For example, if your epileptoid friend tells you that he is having a problem with

ABC and you feel that he is trying to get you to offer your help, then do not. Wait until he directly asks for it as epileptoids have a very nasty habit of saying, *"I did not ask you to do that for me"*.

For instance, assume that you have offered him your help without him directly asking for it, then the probability that he will take it for granted is huge. Also, let us assume that you ask him for a favor in the future or you feel that he is being unfair to you for some reason, and you remind him of the past favor that you have done for him. Then he will easily get away by saying "*I did not ask for your help, you offered it yourself*".

Last but not the least, **never sacrifice your own comfort for epileptoids**. Do not forget that what you do for people affects their belief systems directly. If you sacrifice your own comfort for an emotive, then he will form positive thoughts about you. The same is not true for epileptoids. They will start thinking that "*this is how it is supposed to be*" or "*this person must always do this for me*". Nonetheless, such beliefs in epileptoids do not develop after one or two favors, rather, from the accumulation of iterative and similar favors.

I would like to give a personal example for this. Once I landed an internship position at one bank in Azerbaijan. It was during the summer after the first year of my undergraduate degree. All of my colleagues were competitive though friendly people, and the head of our team was an epileptoid. My colleagues were used to leaving the workplace after 6 pm, even if there were some tasks left to do. They would basically do them the next morning.

During my first two months, I decided to differentiate myself, and therefore, I stayed late until 8 or 9 pm and never left before completing all of the tasks that were either assigned to me individually or as a part of the team. However, seeing that none of my teammates ever cared to overstay and help me to complete what was supposed to be "our" tasks, I got overwhelmed and decided to leave at 6 pm from that time on. This situation ended badly for me. Not knowing back then what I know now, by sacrificing my own comfort in order to get respect and appreciation in the workplace, I have, unfortunately, created a malicious belief system in the minds of all people in our department, which was:

"Salim is the one who is responsible for staying late and completing the team's tasks. This is the reason why he was hired"

What happened next? Well, during the next day, when my epileptoid boss opened his laptop at 8 am and saw that "leverage checks" were not ready, he stormed off from his office and exploded at all of us. He was irritated and asked, "*why the hell are leverage checks not ready?*". At that moment, one of my colleagues gave me a good life lesson when he stood up from his desk and said, *"Salim was supposed to stay late and complete them"*. Of course, I ended up being condemned for it. Unsurprisingly, I was condemned in a standard epileptoid way, i.e., I have been labelled as someone so selfish and careless that he preferred to leave the job early instead of staying and helping the team.

I felt extremely anxious and furious at that moment. Before joining the company, the leverage checks were never ready at 8 am in morning. It was me, who stayed late time after time, completing these checks and sending them at 9 pm daily, for our "dear" boss to see them done in the morning. And what did I get in return? Public humiliation.

However, seeing that my teammates abandoned me, I decided to make their lives miserable by ensuring that all of us from that time on stayed late and completed those checks. From that moment on, I never volunteered for any tasks that would affect people's perception of me so that they would start exploiting me.

Nonetheless, I still take huge initiatives in my workplace, but I ensure that I will be differentiated or rewarded by completing those initiatives — no free-riding from now on.

Alcohol and Drugs

It is frequent to observe that epileptoids incline towards alcohol due to their tension and stress. After the first few rounds of drinks, they feel the urge to carry on until blacking out. Epileptoids usually prefer drinking vodka and similar drinks with higher alcohol rates. They also prefer cigarettes with stronger rates of nicotine. Taking in the high potency of alcohol is the figurative approach adopted by epileptoids to manage their anger or soothe their overwhelmed state of mind.

In a sober state, epileptoids act within certain borders of seriousness, toughness, and stiffness, while quite the opposite is observed under the influence of alcohol. Actions while under the influence are often performed automatically, and an epileptoid himself cannot comprehend his own actions. The friendly and non-distant behavior under the influence surprises all around him. However, epileptoid will feel bothered if he remembers his actions once sobering up as he will be feeling internal discomfort and external shame.

Luckily for epileptoids, amnestic forms of alcoholism are highly frequent, that is, an epileptoid will have no memory of what happened during his time under the influence. Although some forms of memory loss are common for all individuals after the alcohol intake, the severity of this is quite distinguishable in epileptoids.

For that reason, people around him should not allow any experiences from the drunk state to affect their relationship. For example, an epileptoid may act much friendlier and carelessly under the influence of alcohol, which might impact the people around him to act much friendlier and carelessly when he is sober. However, epileptoid will become irritated from this, which will lead to an explosion of anger if the situation escalates. Thus, we should not take any actions of epileptoids under the influence as a sign that the nature of the relationship has changed.

An epileptoid, under the influence, may say that you are his best friend, but he will not admit to it when sober. Furthermore, it is not uncommon to observe epileptoids performing crazy acts under the influence of alcohol. For instance, they may get naked from head to toe, kiss someone out of nowhere, strip dance, and much more. I have observed one epileptoid getting completely naked and running down the street after getting drunk. My friends and I caught and dressed him before he blacked out. Interestingly, he did not remember any of this after he woke up.

Epileptoids are far less likely to consume drugs apart from alcohol or nicotine. This comes directly from their fear of becoming a drug addict that could have a long-term negative impact on their lives. Epileptoids fear uncertainty. The uncertain effects of drugs are something they fear. For example, they are uncertain whether they will become an addict after consuming a certain drug, but because the cost of consuming is addiction, they decide not to. But in this case, why do they consume alcohol?

Well, epileptoids are the best examples for people with standard-thinking. Because alcohol consumption is legal and many people around the world consume it repeatedly, epileptoids do not fear it. That is to say, they apply the concept of *"social proof"* when consuming alcohol. But take cocaine, for example. It is an illegal drug, and it is possible to have a heart attack from it, even after the first dose. It is a widespread knowledge that it is a highly addictive drug with hazardous effects on health. And because many people fear it as well, epileptoids do not incline to it. They apply the concept of *"social proof"*.

Nonetheless, epileptoids are likely to consume drugs that are less dangerous to their health, and there is somewhat noncritical public opinion behind it. One common example would be marijuana. It is common for epileptoids to smoke weed. But in contrast to their peers, who stop smoking after reaching the euphoric state, epileptoids pursue until they blackout. This is because they want to feel as relaxed as possible.

As you can see, the way they consume drugs is similar to how they consume alcohol – they persist until blacking out. In such cases, their friends may attempt to discourage them from that behavior but any attempt to tear them away or distract them from this habit may be responded with an aggression.

Obsessive-compulsive personality disorder

Now we will study what happens when the epileptoid character accentuates to a pathological state. There is no single DSM or ICD-equivalent personality disorder that would fit such character. But there is one personality disorder that closely resembles it and that is the ***Obsessive-Compulsive Personality Disorder (OCPD)***. I am aware that most of you have probably heard of obsessive-compulsive disorder, generally known as OCD. Note, however, OCD and OCPD are not the same; OCPD is a personality issue, while OCD is a mental health issue.

What are the main signs and symptoms of OCPD? They're extremely similar to what you've studied so far in this chapter but on a much accentuated degree:

- Stiff, tough, and rigid manners

- Attention to detail

- Overwhelming need for punctuality

- Strong obedience to rules and regulations

- Devotion to work, even though it might damage social or family relationships

- Frugality with money

- Strong sense of righteousness

- Strong ownership and desire for complete control over the individual tasks, and so on

As you may recall, all the traits mentioned above are the common personality attributes of epileptoids. Keep an eye out for strong ownership and desire to have total control over individual tasks. Under this condition, do you think that people with OCPD (and epileptoids) would delegate their tasks to someone else? Well, you already know that epileptoids are not the best team players, and they have a strong distrust towards the people. Epileptoids and people with OCPD will never delegate their tasks to others because they'll fear it will not be done correctly.

Both epileptoids and people with OCPD hardly express their emotions because they associate emotionality with weakness. As you can imagine, people whose top priority is maintaining their own safety would not do anything associated with showing weakness. As such, these people do not express their emotions or affections.

As epileptoids, people with OCPD are rigid, stiff, stern, and overconscientious when it comes to ethics and morality. This might be a bit surprising given that epileptoids have a natural tendency to affective explosions, but they always believe that they are right. I have never met any epileptoid who has exploded at someone and, after cooling down, admitted that he was wrong. They have always told me: *"I was right; he was wrong"*.

This is a bit confusing since if you are in the right, how do you justify your behavior of exploding at someone? The answer is simple. Epileptoids feel their affective explosions are justifiable as long as they believe they were right. That is, if you are correct, then you have the right to explode. They feel justified in doing so without considering how deep they can hurt the person in front of them.

Epileptoids do not have perfectionist traits, unlike the people with OCPD. I had a colleague who argued that epileptoids are also perfectionists. His argument was that the perfectionist traits of epileptoids is the main cause behind their inertia. To explain his logic, think of it this way. Perfectionism generates a fear of making mistakes. This fear encourages a person to avoid doing whatever he isn't good at since the chances of making a mistake are greater in areas where you aren't completely competent. My colleague concluded that epileptoids rarely get out of their comfort zone because they fear making mistakes, which arises from their perfectionism. Not leaving your comfort zone, in turn, is one of the key symptoms of inertia.

But he was wrong, and he agreed with me in the end. Let me tell you what I told him. The reason why epileptoids do not embark on doing things that they are not good at is that they do not want to look weak or awkward. They are afraid of embarrassing themselves and losing their credibility. It is not their perfectionism. Indeed, epileptoids are quality-oriented but perfectionism, as a trait, is highly concentrated and simply does not apply to these people.

Both epileptoids and individuals with OCPD have strong principles and strict standards. For this reason, they do not view the world colourfully. Instead, their worldview is polarised and dichotomous (dichotomous means dividing things into two parts). For example, you are either right or wrong, either a friend or an enemy, either a good person or a bad person. There is no grey area that you walk on. Either you are on the right side of things or the wrong side. Indeed, the dichotomy is not a wise character trait, and people with this feature should try and work on it.

Now that you understand OCPD and how closely it resembles the character traits of epileptoids, I would like to compare it to pathological accentuation of epileptoids. The rage, fury, dysphoria, and affective explosions of epileptoids are not observed in individuals with OCPD. In this case, one might suggest that the psychopathological state of epileptoids can be classified as "*OCPD combined with some <u>antisocial features</u>*".

However, ***antisocial personality disorder (ASPD)*** is mainly characterized by the pervasive violation of the rights of others and by a weak or no conscience at all. As you studied throughout the chapter, this is not true for epileptoids. Nonetheless, the rage and explosive state between people with ASPD and psychopathological epileptoids are similar. And in cases of extreme accentuation that reach the level of psychopathy, epileptoids may be diagnosed with antisocial personality disorder.

Influencing and Manipulating Epileptoids

In this chapter, I introduced few techniques of influence and manipulation that you could use with epileptoids. I will start by quickly reinstating them here:

- ***Never give epileptoids the illusion of control***: Do not let epileptoids think that they can command you. Avoid all the circumstances where you could fall under their control. You can do this by ***creating an impression of authority*** or by ***keeping a distance*** with them. It is always best to do both. Do not show them your emotions since they interpret emotionality as a weakness. Furthermore, do not allow them to assign any tasks or responsibilities to you (unless they are your boss). They might attempt to do it directly or indirectly. Thus, once you realize their attempt at this, distance yourself from them. Moreover, **do not do epileptoids any favors** since they take things for granted. This will also help to maintain your distance from them. Finally, **never sacrifice your own comfort for them** since they will get used to it, which will lead them to expect similar favors from you in the future. So, as long as you maintain self-awareness, epileptoids will not assume that they are in charge of you and that they can control you.

- *Character Evidence*: This is a useful manipulation technique that you can use with any psychotype. In times of conflict or disagreement, reminding the person of their past yet similar behavior will rattle them directly. If the seduction technique is the forte of histrionics, then the character evidence technique is the forte of epileptoids. Therefore, do not give epileptoids any material that could incriminate you in the future. You can do this by keeping a certain degree of distance from them.

These were some of the manipulation techniques that I taught you throughout the chapter. The techniques listed below are further ways you can influence and manipulate epileptoids:

- **Commitments**: One of the best ways to influence epileptoids is to get them to make commitments. This is because once they make a commitment, e.g., make a promise, they deliver it. In case they cannot deliver it, even better as you will be able to exploit their guilty conscience by asking for something bigger as some sort of compensation.

- **Control your communication**: When speaking with epileptoids, make sure you stick to the facts. Be detail-oriented but yet succinct and specific. Do not overwhelm them with unnecessary details. Also, refrain from asking too many questions. Unlike what you might have been taught at school, epileptoids do believe that there are stupid questions. In addition, maintain a low voice tone and speak at a normal pace. They will get overwhelmed if you speak fast or skip from one topic to another.

- ***Be pragmatic***: Epileptoids, unlike schizoids, dislike theorizing about things. They have a strong desire to take action. If you're working with them, you should use the same approach.

- ***Be a problem solver***: Epileptoids will love you if you create an impression of a problem solver. Think of it from a logical standpoint. Epileptoids get themselves involved in every problem, and as a result, they get overwhelmed. They are not inclined towards delegating their tasks since they do not trust that others will deliver accurately. If they believe that you are a problem solver, they will respect you, and more likely it will be that they will choose to work with you. Such experiences provide opportunities to develop a strong relationship with epileptoids. However, this does not mean that you should solve their problems without them asking for it or even being aware of it. Do not forget that they are inclined towards taking things for granted and are not the people who would appreciate or admire your work. What you need to do is to have the impression of a reliable person with great problem-solving skills and wait until they ask (or plea) for your help directly.

- ***Create an impression of a reliable person***: Being a problem solver alone is not enough for epileptoids to like you or work with you if they do not think that you are, as they say in streets, *"solid"*. For this reason, always be honest and deliver your promises, i.e., *"be a man of your word"*. Also, if epileptoids observe that you are not fulfilling your commitments towards others, then they will be suspicious of you. They will think that you are faking the role of a *"reliable person"* in order to get what you want. Do not forget, epileptoids are very observant and extremely sceptical. You do not want, in any case, to trigger their suspicion or distrust.

- ***Do not compliment them***: While complimenting and praising histrionics is a good attempt to influence them, the opposite is correct about epileptoids. These people are suspicious, sceptical, and distrustful. This is what they have in common with narcissistics and fanatics. When you praise the members of these psychotypes, they think that you are seeking something. You must refrain from all possible situations where you could trigger the suspicion and scepticism of these people.

- ***Get involved in their interests***: Epileptoids are often involved in sports. You may take advantage of this to spend more time with them. Often, epileptoids are not doing well in sports involving teamwork. For this reason, the areas of sports that they are more involved in include working out, playing table tennis, swimming and so on. Nonetheless, it is possible to observe that some epileptoids enjoy football, basketball or any other areas of sports that involve teamwork. As a result, make the most of the circumstances. Inquire as to whether they'd want you to join them. If they agree, take advantage of the chance to build a rapport with them.

- ***Mirror them***: Remember some of the basic traits of epileptoids: serious, responsible, punctual, tidy, organized, disciplined, analytical, smart and respect for rules and standards. As a result, they appreciate and welcome people who exhibit the aforementioned personality attributes. Remember that epileptoids have a strong sense of righteousness. Therefore, they believe that by possessing these personality traits, they are doing the right thing. If you mirror these qualities, you will be regarded as the right person in their eyes.

- ***Do not overwhelm them:*** Try not to exhaust them with many flows of information. They quickly get overwhelmed when they hear or observe many things.

- ***Ensure their safety:*** Epileptoids value safety and stability above everything else. As a result, avoid doing anything that can make them feel threatened

Conclusion

In the chapter for histrionics, I attached the mnemonic developed by H. Pinkofsky. I intend to do the same for epileptoids. I will use the mnemonic for OCPD: "LAW FIRMS:"

L	Loses point of activity due to preoccopuation with details
A	Ability to complete tasks, though compromised by perfectionism
W	Worthless objects (unable to discard anything)
F	Friendships and leisure activities are excluded due to preoccupation with work
I	Inflexible, scrupulous and overconscientious on ethics, values, or morality which are not accounted for by religion or culture
R	Reluctancy to delegate tasks
M	Miserly towards self or others
S	Stubborness and rigidity

Now that you have learned epileptoids in great detail, it is time to summarize it and move on to our next psychotype, hyperthymics. The chart below summarizes the key characteristics of the epileptoid psychotype:

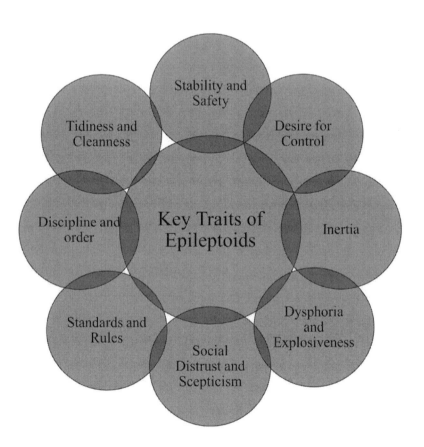

4

Hyperthymics

"Whenever I am with energetic young people, I feel like a recharged battery"

(Nelson Mandela)

Hyperthymic means "high spirited" in Greek. As if Nelson Mandela used the aforementioned words to describe hyperthymics. As the name suggests, such people are "hyped", meaning that they are very energetic, active, positive and adventurous. They love surrounding themselves with a lot of people. Mostly, these people are optimistic, and they can find positivity almost on any occasion. Hyperthymics are future-oriented and agents of change. Hence, they welcome and approach all innovations with extreme enthusiasm. This is a trait that hyperthymics have in common with histrionics. However, there is a difference.

Histrionics welcome changes that are facilitated by them. That is to say, histrionics are in the favor of a novelty only if it was initiated by them. Hyperthymics, on the other hand, do not care much about who initiated it. This is because they do not care who takes the credit as long as they have fun. They are not as self-centred as histrionics.

When speaking to hyperthymics, you can see the enthusiasm in their eyes. Their immense eagerness, adventurousness and curiosity pushes them towards many experiences. They approach everyone with keen and sincere interest. The high-spiritedness and elevated mood of hyperthymics lead to high vitality, glowing appearance and a great feeling of oneself. They always have a good appetite and a healthy sleep. Due to being energetic and active, they are involved in nocturnal activities. Even if they get a little sleep, which is often the case, they wake up in the morning with a good degree of energy. They can maintain a sizable degree of mental and physical energy for prolonged periods of time. But there is one thing that will definitely drain their energy: *Inertia*. Like histrionics, hyperthymics hate inertia. In contrast to epileptoids or hypothymics, physical idleness or lack of physical activities exhaust the energy of these people very quickly.

Hyperthymics

Hyperthymics who are extremely adventurous and curious in nature end up in many unfavourable situations. The phrase *"wrong place, wrong time"* probably applies the most to hyperthymics. But on the positive side, since hyperthymics are highly adaptive (a trait arising from their fast nervous system), they quickly adopt manners, customs, behaviour, style and hobbies of new groups that they get themselves into. However, the high degree of energy and adventurousness inhibits hyperthymics to be confined only within one group.

Due to their vivid curiosity, hyperthymics constantly chase something. They are greedy when it comes to experiencing something new – nothing will ever satiate them. For this reason, hyperthymics cannot develop genuine relationships since they embark on new journeys very quickly. As such, they have many but superficial friends.

Since their childhoods, hyperthymics are distinguished through their energetic mood, social behavior, great mobility, considerably degree of talkativeness, extreme sense of independence and obvious tendencies towards creating mischiefs. But any hallmark of a young hyperthymic is a non-distant behavior towards adults.

In other words, hyperthymic children lack a sense of distance in relation to adults and elders. They do not understand that some jokes should not be made with grownups. It is simply inappropriate. For this reason, parents of hyperthymics try to restrain them as much as possible when they are having over guests. Imagine, a hyperthymic child may easily glue the chair of a visiting guest as he will receive a great deal of enjoyment from it. Hyperthymics enjoy such jokes, and they do not think whether their mischiefs cause discomfort to others.

But hyperthymics never intentionally cause mischiefs that could cause serious physical injury to someone. Instead, they enjoy causing small troubles that would not cause serious or permanent harm. The non-distant behavior of hyperthymics ensues in their adulthood as well. I have many hyperthymic friends who cannot comprehend the idea of personal distance. I have had many of them kissing and touching me inappropriately (not sexually, though) or showing their genitals (this is sexual), just for the fun of it. I have been a miserable victim of immense visual traumas because of my hyperthymic friends.

It is easy to figure out if your child is hyperthymic by paying attention to the amount of noise they make. However, this noise should not be coming from their anger or capriciousness, as in this case, your child could be an epileptoid or histrionic. Instead, the noisy behavior of hyperthymic children derives from them being overly energetic and adventurous. Hyperthymics love surrounding themselves with their peers since they enjoy the company of like-minded people, and they lead them towards action and adventure, and of course, to mischiefs.

When hyperthymics start going to school, they get differentiated by their liveliness and ability to grab everything on the fly. On the downside, however, they exhibit insufficient degree of attention and discipline. As such, they grow through their classes unevenly, e.g., sometimes they score at the top of the class, and on the other times, they score at the bottom. The high degree of excitability is a known inhibitor of performance in academia. Once they reach puberty, the degree of such excitement stabilises over time. They begin developing discipline and attention towards important things but still are extremely social, friendly, joyful and adventurous outside their academic and professional lives.

I think this degree of introduction is enough. This time, we will take a slightly different approach and start from the social relationships of hyperthymics, instead of their thought process.

Social Relationships

Hyperthymics have a wide inner circle, and they establish pleasant relationships with everyone around them. Hyperthymics are the best among all psychotypes in establishing contact with strangers. Their irrepressible interest in everything that happens around leads them to be very welcoming of others. Anything new, e.g., new people, new places, new objects, attracts hyperthymics because of their sincere interest in these things, not because they want to appear as interesting to others.

Random meetings with strangers do not cause any concern for these people, and they strive towards places where all the action is. This is due to their curious, adventurous and dynamic behavior. Also, due to being friendly, social, fun and energetic, people feel drawn to hyperthymics. Hyperthymics spread their positivity faster than the coronavirus – their positivity is contagious. People feel their moods elevated in the presence of hyperthymics, and it is common to witness that the mood of any environment changes when a hyperthymic joins or leaves.

It was mentioned that vivacious histrionics have so much in common with hyperthymics that they can be called as *"histrionics with hyperthymic tendencies"*. The members of these two psychotypes share so many personality traits that taking a vivacious histrionic for a hyperthymic is an easy error to make. But gladly, there is an obvious behavior pattern that expose vivacious histrionics.

Like hyperthymics, vivacious histrionics are entertaining, friendly, fun and witty. They come up with dozens of jokes and entertain everyone around. However, hyperthymics do it for everyone to have a great time. Indeed, they enjoy listening to the wits and jokes of others and receive a great pleasure from it. They do not attempt to dominate the conversation or be at the center of stage. This is not their motive.

Vivacious histrionics, however, are different in this regard. They do not treat the people in the group as their "equals" or partners in conversation. They treat them as their audience. For this reason, they dominate the discussions. They want to be the centre of attention. They do not give others any chance to speak, crack a joke or express an opinion. They do it all themselves.

Do not forget, all histrionics crave attention and display exhibitionist or attention-seeking behaviors one way or another. Of course, such an attitude exhausts and irritates everyone around. They do not allow anyone to speak. Whenever someone attempts at taking the stage, he gets interrupted and swallowed by a vivacious histrionic. By paying attention to such a behavior, you can distinguish a hyperthymic from a vivacious histrionic.

There is another way which you can use to distinguish between hyperthymics and vivacious histrionics. Pay attention to their speech! Do not forget, histrionics have a great fantasy and constantly come up with things that never occurred. When talking about their experiences, they make up a lot of stuff. They do so to make their experiences sound fascinating. Indeed, an interesting story attracts attention, which histrionics crave for.

Hyperthymics are a bit different in this regard. Although they might paint the story up a little bit to make it more presentable and interesting, they do not make up stuff just to get the attention. They tend to share their experiences in an exciting way, but they do not make up lies for it.

Nonetheless, hyperthymics, just like histrionics, have a shallow and superficial attitude due to their fast nervous system. Also, both these psychotypes have a low degree of self-reflection. But hyperthymics are even worse than histrionics when it comes to self-reflection. In fact, hyperthymics have the lowest degree of self-reflection among all people. The reason is that their nervous system is also strong, i.e., people with a strong nervous system are less likely to doubt themselves or look for guilt in their actions. As such, hyperthymics simply do not have a mental mechanism that reminds them of their actions or questions whether something that they did was wrong.

So, many people view hyperthymics as people who lack a sense of empathy. And this is actually true. Hyperthymics rarely think about the feelings of others, and they hardly notice the suffering of their close friends and family members. But this is not due to them not caring about others or due to being unkind — quite the opposite. Hyperthymics are kind, and they hardly refuse the requests of others, but only if the demanded request is something that a hyperthymic can fulfil. Thus, at their core, hyperthymics are not selfish or egocentric, but rather generous and kind.

The kindness of hyperthymics is sincere – one thing they have in common with emotives. When committing good deeds, these people do not think whether it is going to be noticed or appreciated. They do good to others in such a way that a person does not even know from whom it came. Approaching hyperthymics in a friendly and positive manner will result in a great conversation because these people reply to goodness with goodness. Take a step towards them; they will take two towards you. Nonetheless, it does not mean that there is an opportunity for a long-term friendship. Hyperthymics are very superficial in their friendships. The next morning, he is not going to even remember you. Simply put, out of the sight – out of the heart.

Hyperthymics are extremely sexual with almost no boundaries. They enjoy kinky and erotic acts and welcome all forms of sexuality. Often, hyperthymics have bisexual tendencies as a result of their immense interest and desire.

Hyperthymics do not develop genuine emotional feelings towards their sexual partners. They develop temporary love and affection towards every partner, but this lasts until the ejaculation. Afterward, they lose their interest in the person, at least until they are ready for the next round.

Deep love and commitment are not hallmarks of hyperthymics; these traits mostly belong to emotives. Hyperthymics are very prone to cheating on their partners, and they do it with random people at random times. For instance, if a histrionic cheats with someone who admires him, an epileptoid with someone who he admires and a fanatic with one who is needed for reaching his target, a hyperthymic does it randomly.

Hyperthymics

Being highly energetic, hyperthymics get themselves involved in every sort of sport that is available to them. Commonly, they get involved in those sports where most of the people around them are involved in as well. The reason behind this is to have someone to enjoy it with. Due to engaging in sports, hyperthymics own an athletic body type. These people take good care of their appearance and look relatively younger compared to their peers. It is also frequent to observe that hyperthymics attract the sexual or romantic interest of others by exhibiting their athletic skills.

An active facial expression adds dexterity, brilliance and positiveness to hyperthymic's appearance. Since hyperthymics have a fast-nervous system, they use their mimicries quickly. Their basic emotions include excitement, surprise, and wonderment.

Hyperthymics are highly observant. Every nuance, every novelty intrigues them. Their curiosity can be so high that they can enter your personal zone without any permission. These people fail to understand the concept of personal distance. For example, a hyperthymic can open your bag without your consent. Once seeing that you are staring at him, he will say: *"You do not mind it, do you?"*. Interestingly, he will do so after opening your bag.

Hyperthymics differ in their active gestures and speech. By easily adapting to any atmosphere, they keep their energy in harmony with others. These people are social. It can be the end of the world if they cannot contact people. When going to a new city or a country, either for professional or academic purposes, their main fear is being lonely.

Thought Process

A high degree of self-confidence and self-esteem is natural to hyperthymics. This is because of two reasons: their elevated mood and strong nervous system. There is no reason for someone with high positivity, wittiness, energy and adventurousness to feel bad about himself. A strong degree of self-esteem creates favorable conditions for hyperthymics and helps them to demonstrate their skills and abilities. Indeed, many hyperthymics show themselves to others in a favorable light, something we may consider as "showing off".

This resembles a similarity between the behavior of histrionics and hyperthymics, but we can distinguish the "showing off" behavior between these two based on its nature. Hyperthymics resemble sincerity when demonstrating their talents to others, and they do it with real self-confidence. However, the attempts of histrionics in self-demonstration frequently end up with some degree of awkwardness – they demonstrate more than they really have or more than is necessary (apart from theatrical histrionics, who cope with it perfectly). Histrionics also tend to make things up in their attempts of exhibiting themselves.

But another thing that these two psychotypes have in common is hedonism. Hyperthymics, similar to histrionics, hate inertia and are very active. They seek to enjoy everything that life has to offer, and they do it with a great enjoyment. They desire all forms of activities that increase their pleasure. The elevated degree of sexual preoccupation is one of such desires. The momentary seek of hedonism may end up with hyperthymics engaging in unfaithful endeavours, as was discussed previously.

Hyperthymics are very wishful and enthusiastic about the idea of achieving their goals. But in this case, why are the hyperthymics not very successful in reaching their targets? The reason lies within their nervous system. Hyperthymics have a strong and fast nervous system. People with a fast-nervous system are more enjoyable in social gatherings compared to people with a gradual or slow nervous system. Such people are witty, sociable and funny. However, the fast nervous system inhibits putting in enough time and effort to process information in detail. Also, it leads to a superficial and shallow character. Mostly, people with a such nervous system speak before thinking.

If an epileptoid (who possesses a gradual nervous system) takes enough time to think about what goal should he follow, how and with whom should he follow it, a hyperthymic's approach will be superficial: he will quickly decide on what he wants without even thinking if he has the time, effort or any other form resources to pursue it. As such, hyperthymics are somewhat delusional. Even though hyperthymics look pragmatic, they have a shallow attitude and hence, their attempts in reaching their targets frequently end up in failures.

Hyperthymics are very flexible with their aims – they change them quite often due to frequent failures. The saddest part is that they do not self-reflect. Thus, they fail to understand why they have failed and what they should learn from this. When others ask them, "what went wrong" or "why do you think you could not achieve XYZ", they will come up with many irrelevant and even deceitful excuses. This is another personality trait they share with histrionics.

For this reason, do not rely on hyperthymics if you are partnering, befriending or working with them. Accuracy, frugality and loyalty are by no means the hallmarks of these people. By loyalty, we mean everything that is related to commitments, such as loyalty towards a partner, towards a promise and so on. This is due to the structure of their nervous system. But how does such a nervous system cause such behavior?

The fast nervous system causes superficiality and carelessness. The strong nervous system causes confidence. As such, hyperthymics are confident in their superficial and careless actions. Ironically, they do not recognize it themselves, and it is very hard to convince them otherwise since these people do not enjoy hearing preaches.

So, the combination of a fast and strong nervous system leads hyperthymics to become superficial and careless, which naturally extends to their sense of loyalty as well. However, this is not permanent damage – a hyperthymic may realise this trait about himself and afterward, work on improving it.

Now let us talk about frugality. It would be more accurate to say *"let us talk about prodigality (means spending carelessly)"* since "frugality" is a concept foreign to hyperthymics. First of all, hyperthymics are not good at accounting for their expenses because of their reckless and shallow attitude. In addition, they comfortably borrow money from their friends with no feeling of uneasiness. They ignore the unpleasant and concerning idea of subsequent payments that they will need to make in the future. Although hyperthymics forget to pay off their debts, they will feel remorse and return your debt immediately if you remind them about it.

The same logic applies to their commitments as well. For example, they can easily promise someone while avoiding the disturbing idea of the consequent fulfilment. When hyperthymics make a promise, they are sincere about it, and they promise a lot of things. However, hyperthymics hardly fulfil their promises because they easily get distracted and forget about them. If you remind him of it, he will immediately apologise and beg for your forgiveness, and later, he will start trying to fulfil his promise. So, if you have lent money to your hyperthymic friend or they made you a promise and have not fulfilled it yet, it suffices to remind them of it.

Hyperthymics

So, one of the limitations that hyperthymics have is the inappropriate approach towards their responsibilities or to any sort of commitment, for that matter. They see little to no issue in dodging their responsibilities, delaying their tasks, failing to deliver their promises, etc. Furthermore, they are very careless when taking risks. Hyperthymics should learn the idea of "taking measurable risks".

The members of this psychotype are highly optimistic and positive, but at the same time, they are not analytical. Do not forget, analysis is the trait of people who can set aside a period of time to think things through. This seems to be a strenuous exercise for hyperthymics. Also, since they want to stay positive, they subconsciously disregard any factors that could lead them to failure. Instead of thinking about possible risks and how to mitigate them, hyperthymics prefer ignoring the possibility that a problem could occur. Like an ostrich, hyperthymics bury their heads in the sand. I believe the quote by Sir Joshua Reynolds fits hyperthymics very well:

"there is no expedient in life in which a human would not resort to avoiding the real labor of thinking"

Hyperthymics believe that they will be successful, no matter what. As such, they only focus on the rewards they'll reap in a favorable scenario. Although they believe they can control the situation, they usually fail.

Hyperthymics rarely accept that they failed due to their negligence or carelessness. Due to their fast nervous system, they quickly come up with several excuses. This behavior shows itself when they fail to deliver their commitments as well. For example, a hyperthymic who needs to deliver an important task will bring numerous excuses for his failure and then presume his life as if nothing has happened. He will not think about the damage or inconvenience caused to others as a result of his mistake. Interestingly, hyperthymics genuinely believe that their excuses are reasonable. Therefore, people who do not understand the thought process of hyperthymics treat them as selfish people.

I will give an example of this. Once, I met with one of my friends, and we spent the whole night together in London. Around 11 pm, we decided to leave the Hippodrome, a casino in Leicester square, and proceed with the Empire Casino (just a few buildings away). He told me to wait outside since he needed to stop for WC, and that's exactly what I did.

After waiting for nearly 15 minutes, I went back inside to see what was going on and I found him sitting behind a casino desk and gambling. When I told him that this was a bit disrespectful, he denied it and gave excuses with 100% assurance. Therefore, arguing with hyperthymics on such things is to no avail. They will either agree that they are wrong and take short-term measures to avoid the same behavior (but repeat it again in the future) or deny any fault.

Negativity

Every hyperthymic is known for his high-spiritedness. But certain occasions can lead them towards negativity and indignation that are directly related to their nature. We occasionally observe hyperthymics displaying negative emotions, such as anger, vengeance, irritation or aggression. Nonetheless, these emotions will be short-lived and last for a temporary period of time. The most common thing that leads hyperthymics to indignation is experiencing negativity from others, especially from parents.

Hyperthymics receive constant criticisms and redundant preaches from their parents and close surroundings regarding their superficial, adventurous, careless and risk-loving behaviors. The steep tendencies towards suppressing a hyperthymic's independence leads him into an emotional explosion. Such discharges help hyperthymics to reach comfort and liberation from oppression, especially when they feel that they are being forcibly subdued to someone else's will. For example, hyperthymics with parents who try to limit or "fix" their behavior will see them as people who are trying to subdue them to their own will.

The second frequent cause behind a hyperthymic's indignation arises from the consciousness of his own obvious failures and mistakes. Hyperthymics with shallow, daring and extremely dynamic attitudes get themselves involved in many events. Of course, having a superficial, risk-loving, careless and shallow attitude means that they will make many mistakes down the line. After the accumulation of several unpleasant experiences, they go through a negative self-evaluation process – a period with tons of self-criticism and self-deprecation.

The third frequent factor that leads hyperthymics into a negative state is living under a strictly regulated and disciplinary environment. This causes the greatest of outbursts and irritations in hyperthymics since such situations are not suitable for them. Simply put, their inner energy is too big and too huge in order to be tamed under a strict regulatory regime. In such environments, hyperthymics suffer very badly because they are surrounded by serious, disciplined and uptight people who like to manage them.

In such cases, hyperthymics start feeling sad and alone. They cannot seem to find a place for themselves, and as such, they feel deprived of society. If there is a way to escape this environment and never return, this will be their first course of action. However, if living in such an environment seems to last for a while, then hyperthymics undergo a series of unpleasant personality changes. This is because they cannot act the way they want, and they do not have like-minded peers around them. Under such environments, hyperthymics may even develop depression or other forms of disorders.

Regardless of the cause behind the negative emotional state of hyperthymics, it is crucial to understand that if the period of indignation lasts for a period that may no longer be considered "temporary", then this could lead to significant changes in character. Though rarely, the lasting period of negativity may lead to increased discipline, ambition and not to a superficial, but rather to an adequate attitude. However, this is likely to be caused by two conditions.

Firstly, the cause of indignation has to be arising from self-reflection and self-evaluation. Suppose the cause of indignation is due to constant criticisms, preaches and other forms of oppression from his parents. In that case, it will likely not lead to significant character improvements. To satisfy his parents or liberate himself from their nagging, a hyperthymic may commit to temporary adjustments in his attitude. However, once he fully emancipates and liberates himself from the influence of his parents, he will go back to being the same person he was before.

Secondly, the period of self-reflection and self-evaluation must consist of rational and objective deductions. That is to say, a hyperthymic draws the right lessons from his mistakes and understands that the causes behind his failures were due to his superficiality and carelessness.

Emancipation

Like schizoids, hyperthymics believe that living freely is their right, and they value independence more than anything. But there is a difference between schizoids and hyperthymics in this respect. Schizoids seek independence of thought, meaning that they want to be able to chase their dreams, regardless of how unusual or even weird does the society perceive these.

Hyperthymics, on the other hand, seek physical independence, that is to say, they want to act freely, do whatever they want and whenever they want it. They do not like prohibitions or limitations on their social activities imposed by their parents. For example, a hyperthymic with parents who prohibit late-night activities will see this as a serious problem.

How does this nature of hyperthymics reflect itself in their behavior? Well, first of all, it leads to a bright period of emancipation. Hyperthymic adolescents frequently end up in conflicts with their parents, teachers and those who interfere with their choices. Hyperthymics do not like when someone interferes with their lives – they love the autonomy. Such interferences include control, guardianship, instructions, preaches, moral lessons, criticisms, responsibilities, etc. All such measures only cause an uplift in the resistance and increase the struggle for autonomy and independence. The common ways in which hyperthymics show resistance include heated arguments, disobedience and, in extreme cases, a deliberate violation of rules and regulations.

To be freed from the guardianship of their parents or their caretakers, hyperthymics do various things. For example, they seek the company of their peers and try spending most of their time with them. This reaction is also frequented in histrionics during their period of emancipation. Furthermore, hyperthymics volunteer for social responsibilities among their peers, such as leading a sports team or a society.

Also, due to being social and adventurous, hyperthymics utilize every opportunity to distance themselves from their homes, such as school trips, summer camps, tourist tours and so on. Nonetheless, this does not work well for youthful hyperthymics since they will soon be objected to new regimes and disciplines, which will inevitably cause some sort of collision.

There is one more thing that inspires hyperthymics to resist and violate rules apart from the emancipation. *Their frivolousness.* What is forbidden is enticing. If you want a hyperthymic to perform a specific action, it is enough to forbid it.

For instance, if you want your hyperthymic child to read a certain book, just tell him that he cannot read that book. Shortly after this, your son will start secretly reading it. Hyperthymics enjoy the rush of adrenaline when they are going against the rules. They simply cannot resist the urge. This temptation is so strong that it even justifies any outcome or punishment once a hyperthymic gets caught.

Influencing and Manipulating Hyperthymics

Hyperthymics despise any type of restriction, criticism, or preaching, and they react negatively to them. If you want to influence someone, you must never allow your connection to deteriorate. So, do not criticise or reproach hyperthymics for their shallow, thoughtless, and careless behaviors. You might assume that they will find sense in your words, reflect on them and understand you, but they will simply ignore you. When confronting a hyperthymic on his careless attitude, he will not understand you at all. Assume that you tell him: *"you are being late to work every single day! You should stop doing so or the boss may find out"*. In this case, he will likely reply as: *"do not worry, I will try to make it so that the boss never finds out"*. As you can see, he does not understand that the problem is his reckless behavior, not whether the boss learns about it or not. For this reason, do not preach hyperthymics as it is not going to work.

Instead, hyperthymics value kindness, understanding, and sincerity, so you have to adopt these behaviors when interacting with them. They are not the best listeners, and for this reason, do not share your sorrow or disappointment with them. They will hardly be helpful. Instead, try to portray yourself as a person who is always positive, genuine, polite, active, witty and whimsical, and fun to hang out with. This way, hyperthymics will naturally approach you and even chase you.

It is hard to maintain such a relationship with hyperthymics where you have frequent get-togethers because they will exhaust you. These people want to engage in all forms of activities and keeping up with them will be challenging. So, do not tag along with them because you will get exhausted, and hyperthymic will notice this and get bored of you as well.

Instead, there is a relationship technique that you can use, which I devised purely for hyperthymics. These people forget about their friends very quickly. As said previously, out of sight – out of the heart. Regardless of how frequently you meet up with them, they will easily forget about you. But if you reduce the number of meetings with hyperthymics and increase the quality instead, they will start chasing you.

To increase the quality of your time with hyperthymics, try to be as interesting as possible. Firstly, learn about the recent things that happened in areas that interest your hyperthymic friend, e.g., if he is a Manchester City fan, then learn about the results of recent games, transfers, and news concerning that club. This way, you will have something interesting to talk about with your friend throughout your time together. Perhaps Manchester City or even the football itself does not interest you. Perhaps you do not want to talk about these at all. Maybe you want to talk about classical music or opera. But it does not matter what you want to talk about. All you have to want is to influence them. And to influence people, we need to be aware of their interests and be able to contribute to the conversation around these topics.

Secondly, plan multiple events for the time you will spend together. Hyperthymics are very active and dynamic, so they do not like spending all their time sitting at one place. It is a better idea to plan at least 3 things that you will do during the night, such as going to a pub to get some drinks first, then to an attraction park or a polygon (though do not do this after drinks) and then to a casino perhaps. Or you could go to a bar, where you can meet random people who already had one too many and are in the mood of conversating with strangers.

Overall, if you act this way, you'll give your hyperthymic friend an interesting and adventurous night, and he'll definitely want to meet you again. And as your relationship improves, so will the degree of your influence on your friend.

Conclusion

Among all people, hyperthymics are the most positive and independent. Like schizoids, they do not care about what others think of them, which frees them from an immense psychological burden. They determine their own path of life and live by their own rules – the trait that I've always admired about hyperthymics so that I have adopted it myself. I suggest you to do the same.

5

Conformals

"Conformity is the jailer of freedom and the enemy of growth"

(John F. Kennedy)

Conformity was traditionally studied as a personality trait rather than a psychotype. However, there are such people who conform to the behavior of their surroundings so significantly that conformity becomes their fundamental character trait. And the number of such people has been increasing quite considerably in the last few decades. As such, it makes a lot of sense to classify these people as "conformals" and study them under a unique psychotype.

You will first begin by studying what conformity is and how it is taught in the field of psychology. The main thing to understand from here is that all people have a certain degree of conformity. But as someone who wants to read people, you need to determine the degree of conformity in every person you meet. The first part of this chapter will help you with this. Afterward, you will learn about the conformal psychotype and acquire the knowledge and skills necessary to read them. Having said that, let's begin.

Conformity

To begin with, conformity, for an individual, is his tendency of aligning his behavior, habits, values, views, beliefs, and attitudes with his social environment. As human beings, we all possess a certain degree of conformity, and this is something good and valuable. For instance, we all develop certain eating habits beginning from our childhood. As we grow, we align our eating habits with that of the general public so that when we dine outside, people do not stare at us blankly and try to guess from which cave we have emerged. Simply, we are adopting the generally accepted eating habits of society. This is how we are conforming towards a certain habit of the public.

Why do we have a certain degree of conformity? Because as much as we value our privacy and uniqueness, we also value how others perceive us. Humans are social creatures. We all want to be respected, admired and approved. We do not want to display an image of ourselves that alienates and isolates us from society. Therefore, conformity is a natural character trait of all humans, and it is a very important and useful attribute. It is also a tool for adaptation. Individuals with low degrees of conformity can hardly tolerate changes in their environments. Such instances could lead to severe failures.

I would like to give an example. I lived my whole life in Azerbaijan until I got accepted to King's College London and came to the U.K. to study economics. I was 16 years old back then. I had a friend from Azerbaijan who also got accepted to the same degree, and we came to London together. But he endured severe problems in adapting to the new environment. The cultural differences were significant, and he simply lacked conformity. He could not establish any form of relationship with anyone for the duration of the entire course. He could not make any friends because he could not adapt to the mentality and the diverse views of people in London – he simply could not demonstrate traits in his personality that conformed with the culture and mentality of people living here. And this, eventually, made him want to leave. I remember him having dreams of staying in the U.K. and working in the field of macroeconomic research, but in the end, he returned back to Baku.

Therefore, conformity is a necessary and useful trait if we want to adapt to a new environment. But I would say that the most useful benefit of conformity is that it provides us with a shortcut when making decisions. We usually tend to act the way that is deemed appropriate by society. We look at the actions and behaviors of others when trying to decide what the right course of action is. Religion is one of the best examples of this. We start adopting a certain religion since our childhood, and most often, this is the religion to which the majority of the people surrounding us belong. We do not study every single religion and think of what attracts us the most – we simply choose the one that our social environment belongs to, i.e., our parents, friends, educators, and family members. We take a shortcut – we conform.

This implies that there are instances when we observe the actions and views of our imminent surroundings and then use conformity as a decision-making tool. As such, conformity is a tool of influence. Robert Cialdini, in his book "Influence", demonstrated the influential side of conformity in the chapter called "Social Proof". I have mentioned this technique previously, but I have not linked it to conformity up until now. I cannot say whether Cialdini himself was aware of such a link. But the notion of conformity supports his theory on "social proof".

As said earlier, conformity can be used as a shortcut when making choices, and of course, human beings tend to take these shortcuts as it makes their lives easier. Indeed, thinking through every choice is a tricky process. Instead, it is much easier to pursue an existing path that others thought, developed, and followed. If the outcome was favorable for others, then we are likely to follow it as well. If the outcome was unfavourable, then we condemn it and pledge never to follow it.

However, this is a curse as well. When it comes to deciding what sort of life we want to forge, we have to self-reflect and understand ourselves. To do so, we have to distance ourselves from conformity, at least until we decide what we want. And this might be very difficult for someone who abused such shortcuts throughout his life.

It is important to understand that while these shortcuts are useful here and there, we cannot rely on them for every decision we make. We have to avoid getting addicted to them. We might just block the channels in our brain that support independent and creative thinking. Indeed, people with a high degree of conformity naturally lack creative and analytical thinking skills. They also fail to form rational judgements.

Now that you've familiarised yourself with the benefits of conformity (which are many) and the potential risks, let's introduce some technical concepts and develop a structured understanding of conformity. I promise I will not make it too technical.

Any individual is influenced to conform with the norms, views, and behavior of the society through two channels:

1) ***Normative Social Influence***: This is when we agree or conform to a certain belief or behavior in public while privately disagreeing with it or not accepting it. We do so in order to avoid punishment or get a reward. For example, in the presence of radicals, you may agree or refuse to refute certain viewpoints in order to avoid conflict. Or we can laugh at the obviously-not-funny joke of someone with the sole purpose of not hurting his feelings.

2) ***Informational Social Influence***: This is when we agree or conform to a certain belief or behavior in public so that we can act appropriately or avoid standing out. This is also a shortcut in decision-making that I discussed earlier. For example, when deciding what the best diet is, we rarely go to a dietician. Instead, we google *"how to*

lose 10 kilos in a month" and read the stories of people who have tried some diet and somehow succeeded. We then find ourselves performing that diet (well, at least until we get hungry). Such conformity is our natural habit. We tend to believe that what worked for others will work for us as well.

Now that we know why we have a certain degree of conformity, let us study the degrees of conformity. According to Herbert Kelman, there are three levels of conformity:

1) ***Compliance*** – the lowest degree of conformity

2) ***Identification*** – a moderate degree of conformity

3) ***Internalisation*** – the highest degree of conformity

When our conformity towards a certain action or belief is at the degree of *compliance*, we conform to a specific action or belief when we are in public, but we do not perform or agree to it privately. That is to say, we behave in a certain way only when we are in the presence of someone. Also, it is a temporary phenomenon; that is, we are likely to abandon such habits and beliefs in the long term.

For example, assume you are in a certain group that idealises Donald Trump. Also, assume that you dislike him. In this case, you are more likely to keep your negative views on Trump to yourself for as long as you are in that group. This can also be viewed as the normative social influence of conformity.

When our conformity towards a certain action or belief is at the degree of *identification*, then we are conforming to that action or belief when we are both in public and in private. But it is also a temporary phenomenon. It is something that we are likely to abandon when our environment changes. This case is frequently observed when we start idealising someone. We start adopting that individual's behavior and views, and we perform them both privately and publicly. However, once our idealization ends, we start to abandon those views and behaviors.

Finally, when our conformity towards a certain action or belief is at the degree of *internalization*, we conform to that specific action or belief both privately and publicly, and it is a permanent phenomenon. This is such belief or action that we have conformed to both privately and publicly and that we will keep it in the long-term, or maybe for the rest of our life. Religion is a perfect example of this.

The table below summarizes the three levels of conformity:

	Is the behavior exhibited publicly?	Is the behavior exhibited privately?	Will the behavior last for long-term or short-term?
Compliance	Yes	No	Short-term
Identification	Yes	Yes	Short-term
Internalisation	Yes	Yes	Long-term

Conformity is a broad topic. And, as much as I'd want to study it here in detail, it would be counterproductive to the purpose of this book. Nonetheless, I believe the content taught was more than sufficient for the general understanding of this trait. So, let us begin studying the conformal psychotype.

Conformal Psychotype

Conformals tend to think like everyone. They develop life principles that correspond to principles of their immediate surroundings. As such, they are quite vulnerable to peer pressure. They hardly have any unique views or ideas. The degree of individualism and narcissism is rarely observed in these people. As long as they belong to a certain group, they neither tolerate steep changes in their behavior nor attempt to demolish stereotypes that they have. Therefore, they tend to be stubborn, and their perception of life becomes extremely rigid and severely limited by the worldviews of their immediate surroundings.

Rigidity, stubbornness, and the dislike to be distinguished are some traits that conformals have in common with epileptoids. But in contrast, conformals are friendly and refrain from conflicts. This is obvious if we think of it logically. Will someone whose main approach consists of conforming to others get involved in a conflict? No, of course.

The conformal character begins developing from childhood. A child begins agreeing with everything that the nearest surroundings offer. He agrees with the teachings of his parents and educators and follows their rules. But once he falls into a certain peer group, he starts changing his attitude and begins adapting to a new set of views and attitudes. Conformal teenagers, therefore, do not develop their own "self" since they lose their attitude towards the events happening around them. Conformal's assessment of the world becomes entirely aligned with his peers – those he is constantly communicating with.

But it is in our natural instinct to adopt the views and attitudes of our peers. And conformity is a natural character trait. As such, how would you determine whether a person merely resembles conformity traits (that are natural to human beings) or is a member of conformal psychotype?

Conformals

Well, every conformal is distinguished by his constant and excessive adaptability to his immediate environment and almost total dependence on a certain group to which he belongs. The main worldview of conformals is to follow the herd mentality. This applies to a wide variety of areas, including clothing, behavior, attitude, values, beliefs and views, even on the most important issues. These people are tied to a group of peers and unconditionally accept the values of that group, whatever those values are, without any thought or criticism. As such, conformals are very vulnerable towards being victims of serious crimes if they have been involved in delinquent groups. As a result, their immediate future is largely determined by the nature and direction of their present group.

What are the attractive personality features of conformals? First and foremost, these people are friendly. They are not sources of conflict or discord, as they accept the lifestyle of the group without any criticism. Communicating with people is easy for conformals, though the extent of their relationship would depend on the group's approval to which they belong.

Conformals are very compromising in nature. They do not volunteer to any positions of leadership. Instead, they want to be led. They agree with the proposals of their immediate surroundings and willingly participate in their adventures.

But on the downside, these people lack the courage and determination to follow their own passions. Lack of self-sufficiency, wilfulness and almost complete lack of self-criticism and criticism of his immediate surroundings are among the most unfavourable character traits in conformals. The saddest part is that people view conformals as uninteresting – even their friends view them as ones who are ready to obey but have little to offer.

Self-reflection of conformals is inadequate; they swim in the current, blindly obey their friends and follow the herd mentality. Society thinks and acts for them; hence, the quality of their life is limited to imitation. Remember, conformals always desire to align themselves with their immediate surroundings, and they can hardly resist this urge. Therefore, an individual with a conformal psychotype will be entirely a product of his microsystem. In a good environment, conformals become good. But when they get into a bad environment, they gradually master all the filthy customs, habits, manners and behaviors, regardless of how contrary these are to everything they possessed beforehand, regardless of their harm and danger.

Entrepreneurship and initiation are not among the quality traits of conformals. This is something they have in common with rhapsodics. Members of these two psychotypes hardly take initiative or risks. Instead, they obey the norms of society and follow a life path that has been already followed by many. Moreover, they are likely to work for the same company for a prolonged period of time, even if they do not get fairly promoted. People may view this behavior of conformals and rhapsodics as being loyal or being stupid, but it is neither. Simply, these people struggle to think independently and rationally.

The steep changes in their surroundings are not welcomed by conformals since the idea of adapting to a new environment is troubling. Even though conformals are great at adapting to new things, they start thinking about all the burdens they will have to endure and all the problems that could happen if they commit to a change. This is another behavior that distinguishes them from epileptoids. Remember, although epileptoids do not tolerate changes as well, it is due to their inertia – they do not want to bother to change because they are overwhelmed. An epileptoid will indeed commit to as many changes as necessary until he reaches comfort. Also, he will never expose himself to people that might cause harm to him.

As said before, self-reflection of conformals is pretty low since conformance is a trait combined with a remarkable lack of criticism and analysis. All that is said in their familiar environment, all they learn through their usual channel of information, is the truth for them. Even if the information received is clearly not true but comes from the conformal's group, he will accept it as the truth. Lack of self-reflection, creative thinking and innovativeness lead conformals to become conservative in nature. They do not like new things, and they do not like changes. As such, conformals love an established order and a stable environment.

Interestingly, the lack of affection for the new things breaks out with the irrational dislike of strangers. This applies to a newcomer who has joined the group, a representative of another environment or another nationality. Consequently, conformals are not naturally the most welcoming people, and they face hardships in accepting and welcoming diversity. Remarkably, this is another way to distinguish conformity (as a trait) from a psychotype. People who possess healthy traits of conformity are good at welcoming diverse views and adapting to them if this action promises a benefit. But members of the conformal psychotype do not think or behave as such.

Although conformals are friendly and compromising in nature, they have a significant degree of caution and mistrust towards strangers. They take the views, beliefs and attitudes of strangers with doubt, especially if they contradict the views and beliefs of their own group. For example, if a new member joins the group with a different clothing style, the conformal will be the first to criticise it. However, once the majority of the group starts adopting the new clothing style, as will the conformal, forgetting his previous criticism. Otherwise, he would be standing out from his group members – something that he would definitely not enjoy.

Conclusion

In psychology, conformity is interpreted as the subordination of an individual to the opinion of the group, implying a lower degree of independence and autonomy within such individual.

Banality, conservatism and preparedness to obey the voice of the majority are among the main character traits of conformals. The hallmark of this psychotype is the regular and excessive conformance to the immediate and familiar surroundings. The main quality of conformals is aligning their thoughts and actions towards their immediate surroundings. They try to ensure that they have everything like everyone – from clothes and design of the house, all the way up to worldview and judgments on the most important issues. These people do not want to be distinguished from the groups they conform to, and they avoid standing out.

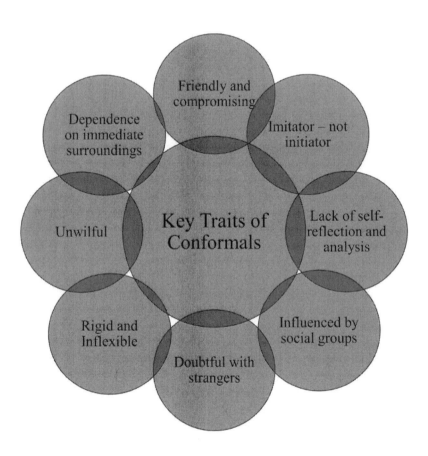

6

Schizoids

"The important thing is not to stop questioning. Curiosity has its own reason for existing"

(Albert Einstein)

You have all met people who are distant from the external world, prefer spending their time in isolation, are facing difficulties in social interactions, and live in their own world. These people also possess a wide curiosity, and everything happening around intrigues them. They also like to think and interpret things in their own ways. Such people, who are also distinguished through their eccentricity, are members of the schizoid psychotype.

Schizoids have a vast inner world; they possess a vivid fantasy and imagination, as well as creative thoughts and views. They are distinguished through their unique perspective on life. They avoid prohibitions at all costs and believe that living independently is their right. They believe that focusing on responsibilities set by others does nothing but impede the quality of living. For them, family and friends are nothing more than the rules of life.

We often see that schizoids perform a certain behavior that does not comply with their age, image or status. Such situations occur often. For instance, a schizoid man of age 30 may act childishly on a certain occasion for no reason, and this behavior will weird out the people around him. However, schizoids do not pay attention to such things – they overlook their actions that look weird, and they do not give any thought as to why they acted the way they did. For example, a schizoid may start bursting out into laughter in a serious environment only because he drifted off and thought of something funny.

Such situations occur often because schizoids live in their own world, i.e., they often get detached from the present life and drift off to various thoughts. Because others do not observe such thoughts of schizoids, the actions of these individuals appear weird. And schizoids overlook such instances in their behavior. But the question is, why do they act on their thoughts?

Schizoids

Many people may drift off to various thoughts that are unrelated to the context or might be awkward. I, for example, tend to fantasize about various things in funerals that would seem extremely awkward or inappropriate, but I do not expose myself as schizoids do. This is because I have intuition and self-awareness. I have a gut feeling which tells me that doing certain things would be inappropriate given the environment. Also, I care how I look from the outside. But if I lacked intuition and self-awareness, then I might also exhibit awkward behaviors while drifting off to various thoughts and fantasies, just like schizoids.

So, there are two reasons why schizoids, when drifting off to various thoughts and fantasies, perform behaviors that may seem inappropriate, awkward or weird given the environment:

1) Schizoids act the way they feel without thinking about how they look from the outside. This is because they lack external self-awareness.

2) Schizoids lack intuition. This is very important to understand about these people, and I will come back to this later in detail.

The term "schizoid" was coined by the Swiss psychiatrist Eugen Bleuler (1908) to describe the human behavior which gravitates away from the external life towards the inner world. In Latin, schizoid means "split" and indeed, the members of this psychotype often appear as if they are torn away from the world. These people frequently drift off from the present time into their inner realm – their fantasy world. Confession of a schizoid:

"Once, when I was going to work from home, I thought that I had lost my phone. I could not find it even if I looked everywhere. After a few minutes, I had a call from home, and I found my phone in my pocket. I was an idiot for I have not searched my pocket first".

The inner world of schizoid is almost always closed from the eyes of outsiders. Even for those who are close to him or who have known him for so many years, the inner world of a schizoid may remain unknown. As such, the most significant features of schizoids are considered to be isolation, solitude, inability and unwillingness to make contacts, and reduced degree of social interactions. But such traits create a favorable environment for a schizoid to think and imagine.

Schizoids

Albert Einstein has said:

"I came to this conclusion when I investigated my manner of thinking and myself: my imagination, dreams, and fantasies are more valuable for me than all I know"

The idea emphasised in the quote above fits the character of schizoids perfectly. Schizoids differ from others in their unusual thoughts and behaviors. These people value imagination, creative thought, and independent thinking very highly. Einstein, who had his own ideas and views on the realm's existence, was a member of none other than schizoid psychotype.

Schizoids are not the most capable people when it comes to social communications. They find difficulties in getting used to any social setting, and they endure severe obstacles while adapting to a new environment or integrating into it. These people are introverted and are neither facilitators nor initiators of any relationship. A schizoid can be recognized as a child who stands back while other children play, does not gravitate towards his peers, avoids dynamic and noisy social settings, and even while conversing with others, plays the passive role and does not add much to the discussion.

If schizoids do not overcome their social struggles in their childhoods, then these traits strengthen after puberty and last for a lifetime. From the beginning of the puberty period, the character traits of schizoids begin to strengthen, and they start appearing more brightly. Introversion, social isolation, gravitating towards his own inner world, involvement in unusual interests and hobbies – all these traits begin to show themselves more obviously.

Schizoids are notoriously untidy. They are unconcerned with the present day because they often get lost in their thoughts. For instance, it is very common for them to lose track of the calendar, i.e., not knowing whether it is a Monday or Wednesday. Or take a schizoid novelist, for example, who would focus only on developing his book, devoting all of his time and effort to it. As such, he will not care about the tidiness of his clothes, the time of the week, orderliness in his house, and even about his personal hygiene (if the accentuation is extreme, though).

As such, untidiness is very visible in schizoids. It is possible to see it in their house, clothes, hairstyle, and behaviors. You have to pay attention to a man's hairstyle to find out if he is a schizoid or not. If an epileptoid cares a lot about the tidiness, a schizoid feels very relaxed with his uncut and messy hairstyle. Once when I mentioned the untidiness of schizoids in a friend group, one of my schizoid friends agreed with me instantaneously and confessed that he was too lazy to get a haircut and instead wore a hat every day when going somewhere in order to hide how messy his hair looked.

Now that we've covered the basics of schizoids, I'd want to focus on their uniqueness and eccentricity. Eccentricity is defined as unusual or odd behavior. This is a natural trait of schizoids as these people vary from others in their distinctive behaviours and unusual thoughts. Afterward, we'll look at how schizoids lack intuition and study their social interactions before delving further into their thought process.

Eccentricity and Uniqueness

Eccentric behavior is characterized by unusual and odd behaviors. The main personality traits that eccentrics have include lack of conformity, high degree of creativity, immense curiosity, heightened intellectual capabilities, lack of need for approval or admiration of others, high degree of self-assurance, unusual or odd clothing, mischievous sense of humor and introversion.

People usually view eccentrics as weird, and their behaviors can usually be thought of as unnecessary. Eccentrics are quite distinguished through their awkward social behavior and radiantly interesting external appearance. Take S. Dali, for example:

Now that you have acquired some information on eccentricity, I'd like to start talking about the eccentric traits of schizoids in more detail. It is important to understand that not all schizoids can be characterized as eccentrics – something that I will explain later in this part.

For schizoids, the lower degree of interaction with peers is compensated by a higher degree of interaction with their own areas of interest. If mathematics is a subject of interest, a schizoid will then spend most of his time with it. Most schizoids are interested in arts, music, combat, gaming, and coding, among many other things. These people have a wide intellectual curiosity, so everything happening around them is intriguing – something they have in common with hyperthymics. But hyperthymics have a shallow attitude, implying that they will not dedicate themselves to things that attract their attention for a long period of time. Schizoids, on the other hand, will get themselves committed.

Schizoids are very curious about everything that happens around them. In neuro-linguistic programming, there is an 80% – 20% law. Based on this law, a successful individual should spend 80% of all resources on his specialization, while 20% on observing areas of his interest. However, schizoids do quite the opposite – they spend 80% of their time on diverse areas but 20% on their specialization.

Things which may seem to you very simple can easily attract schizoids, and they can spend a lot of hours and days on it. Imagine, I recommended a schizoid friend of mine to watch the T.V. series called "Lilyhammer", which is three seasons long. He finished watching this film in four days by losing touch with everybody and diverting from his responsibilities. Hence, schizoids will not reject spending their whole time on things that get their attention or interest. I also recommend you watch this series, but on the condition that you will limit yourself to one episode per day.

Schizoids who do not spend much time interacting with their friends as children spend a lot of time thinking. This way, they strengthen their intellectual capabilities. These people also prefer the companies of elders, but their interactions are limited to being a listener. Because schizoids do not interact a lot with others, they develop their own views and beliefs on the way things are. After reaching puberty, not only do they become immune to herd mentality, but they also turn against it.

Herd mentality is a term that describes how individuals form specific beliefs and opinions due to the influence of others, such as peers, family members, friends, instructors, and so on. Schizoids do not like accepting or rejecting a certain view only because the majority thinks so. They must certainly reach that conclusion on their own. Consequently, it gets harder and harder to convince schizoids to a different view or to adopt a different behavior after their puberty, and this process strengthens even further as time passes by.

Therefore, you cannot influence or manipulate schizoids using the technique called *"social proof"*. Social proof works perfectly on epileptoids and conformals because these people do not like getting distinguished. So, if you tell an epileptoid or a conformal to accept a certain view only because the vast majority of the society agrees to it, he will agree. But if you do the same with a schizoid, he will bluntly reply that *"the vast majority of society is dumb"*. This was actually a response from one of my schizoid friends when I compared one of his behaviors to the majority and told him that he was wrong.

So, schizoids do not like thinking as other people do. Instead, they make their own interpretations of events. As a result, these individuals are highly creative, innovative, and think outside the box. It's no wonder that schizoids are among the most accomplished scholars and innovators. Based on my evaluation and evaluation of my colleagues, people like Bill Gates, Mark Zuckerberg, Elon Musk, Albert Einstein, Nikola Tesla, Marie Curie, Thomas Edison, Grigorii Perelman, Adam Smith, Karl Marx, and many more are the members of schizoid psychotype.

Very often, schizoids lack any form of conformity towards societal views and beliefs. Schizoids, among all psychotypes, are the ones with the least conformity. You have studied the conformal psychotype in the previous chapter, so you know what the traits of conformity are. Not only do schizoids lack conformity towards the views and beliefs of others, but they also lack conformity towards their appearance as well. For example, dressing for the occasion is an alien concept for schizoids – these people will dress however they like to any event they are invited to.

How do you think schizoids, who are eccentric and lack intuition, look from the outside? You already know the answer. Imagine meeting someone with messy hair and a weird style, looking as if he has not put clothes on his body, but clothes have put him inside themselves. Without a doubt, such an individual belongs to a schizoid psychotype. Schizoids are not the tidiest people; messiness is their hallmark. It seems that style and schizoids are two contradicting terms that do not fit one another. They have a troublesome relationship. Generally, schizoids are very indifferent to their clothing and lag behind fashion. Intellectual schizoids who pay attention to education and science prefer filling their cupboards with books than spending money on any brand shoes or expensive accessories.

So, schizoids do not spend much time thinking about their clothes. Pay attention to how Mark Zuckerberg or Bill Gates dress – very simple and plain, even though they could afford anything. These people are schizoids, and schizoids do not see value in appearing stylish or fashionable. But I have also witnessed some schizoids who are highly stylish. But this was because, for these schizoids, fashion was passion. At times of extreme accentuation of character, schizoids care not about their clothing – I have witnessed such schizoids who do not mind wearing clothes with stains or tears on them. Nonetheless, by challenging the common views of society, these people have pushed us towards improvement.

But it is not often that the social isolation of schizoids is rewarded through the abundant degree of originality, innovativeness, and creativity. The richness of the inner world is not typical of all schizoids, and, of course, there is an element of intelligence and talent to it.

Although it is true that the inner world of all schizoids is filled with fantasy, it will not always lead to success. Not all schizoids develop such thoughts which are rewarding, e.g., thoughts such as nihilism, acosmism, radical scepticism, or even anti-natalism. A belief system equipped with such views will definitely not motivate someone towards success. Also, I have witnessed schizoids with thoughts of escaping the human civilisation in order to seek confinement in nature, such as living alone in a forest, island, or somewhere else.

In today's world, turning your knowledge into practice is tedious, and one needs a lot of connections. For example, Bill Gates has partnered with Paul Allen to found Microsoft, and five years later, he convinced Steve Palmer to drop from Stanford Business School to join the company. Or take Mark Zuckerberg, for example, who partnered with Eduardo Saverin and Dustin Moskovitz to make the company named "Facebook".

Schizoids, who lack skills in social interactions, find it immensely difficult to establish mutually beneficial contacts with people, and this is the most dominant inhibitor in a schizoid's path to success.

To sum up, the success of a schizoid will be primarily contingent on three things:

- Does he possess a certain degree of talent and intelligence?
- Are the thoughts and beliefs of the schizoid beneficial?
- Does he have access to resources required to execute his thoughts, such as network, money, and so on?

Overall, detachment from people, lack of intuition and empathy, and extreme involvement in their fantasy world create a suitable environment for schizoids to advance in fields requiring creativity, such as sciences, technology, arts and crafts, chess and so on. However, if a schizoid has self-detrimental thoughts or lacks resources to progress, then it is likely that he will not grow up to anything meaningful.

Even if a schizoid achieves success in his field, he will always be distinguishable from others in his personal life by a significant detachment and lack of adaptability. In times when a schizoid is exposed to numerous occasions where he has to interact with others, his energy will deplete. In such instances, they will seek complete isolation from the outer world and gravitate towards somewhere where they can be alone with their thoughts.

Social Relationships and Lack of Intuition

It was mentioned that "schizoid" means "split" from Latin, and this name is used to characterize the detachment of these people from the real world. They are among the least emotional people and prefer not responding to things happening around them. This can be viewed as apathy. Schizoids often lack emotion and excitement. They don't seem to care about social interactions. However, they are not totally apathetic since they have a wide curiosity, and a lot of things trigger their thoughts.

Due to the lack of intuition, schizoids exhibit an immense amount of contradictory behaviors. For example:

1) Coldness and subtle sensibility

2) Stubbornness and malleability

3) Wariness and gullibility

4) Apathetic inactivity and assertive purposefulness

5) Unsociability and unexpected friendliness

6) Excessive attachments and causeless hostilities

7) Rational reasoning and illogical actions

8) The wealth of the inner world and the colourlessness of its external manifestations

As you can see from above, there are a lot of traits that schizoids exhibit, but these traits act contrary to each other. We can understand that schizoids lack "inner unity", which is most probable, but most likely not the case. Schizoids know what they do not want to do, and they are also aware of what they want. Therefore, we can explain such traits of character due to *"lack of intuition"*.

For example, most schizoids are pedantic during casual conversations. This is due to their lack of intuition – they cannot understand the purpose of the debate and hence, can easily deviate and concentrate on unnecessary details. That is to say; they can concentrate on contextually-unnecessary or inappropriate formality. Mostly, their speech contains a more-than-necessary number of details, which easily bores the other side. For this reason, people attempt to escape conversations with schizoids after having few experiences with them. Under the influence of alcohol, this trait of schizoids signifies considerably.

Indeed, stilted (pedantic) speech is a common symptom of schizophrenia, and you can observe that schizophrenic individuals share a lot in common with the members of the schizoid psychotype. During social discussions, we typically notice schizoids thinking a lot before replying. This is due to their attempts to express themselves formally and correctly. On the other hand, such conduct is inappropriate during casual interactions since the purpose of such debates, as the name implies, is to be casual. Stilted speech of schizoids can also be easily recognized from the number of corrections they do when the other side speaks.

I will give a personal example of this. I was watching the T.V. series named "Suits" with a schizoid friend of mine, and while I explained the series to him, I was referring to it as "movie", instead of "series". And this guy corrected me every single time I said "movie" instead of "series". At one point, it disturbed my thought flow so much that I forgot what I wanted to say in the first place and ended up in a heated conversation with him about his pedanticism. You can imagine that my friend was a member of the schizoid psychotype.

Schizoid, who owns a chaotic thought, separates his ideas in his brain and then forms comments. Schizoid's opinions differ by the unusual attitude to the events around them. For example, if God is almighty, can he create a stone that he cannot lift? If yes, given that there is a stone he cannot lift, is he still almighty? If not, then he is not a God since God has to be almighty. Indeed, such questions show the attitude of schizoids to the events of life. These ideas can seem very unusual and odd to you, but such instances are very frequent when communicating with schizoids as a result of their eccentricity.

The lack of intuition, in turn, inhibits schizoids from understanding, tolerating, and delivering the emotional expectations of their close ones, such as their partners, friends, and family members. It can also be referred to as the absence of an immediate sense of reality. For example, schizoids cannot empathise with the experiences of others or predict what others desire or want from them. They are indifferent when others praise or criticise them. A schizoid has trouble telling whether someone likes or dislikes him. All of these issues arise as a result of their lack of intuition.

For this reason, ensure that you communicate your needs and desires to schizoids directly and comprehensively. These people are not selfish or narcissistic; they simply lack intuition. When they are told what they should do, they mostly do it or at least attempt it.

What other personality traits arise from a lack of intuition? Well, lack of empathy towards others is the most important. Do not assume that schizoids are sociopathic; it is not like they do not emphasize with others because they do not want to. They do not emphasize simply because it does not cross their mind to do so. They do not know whether it is something they should do. Basically, we can understand that empathy is something that schizoids are radically ignorant of.

Due to lacking empathy, schizoids cannot share the emotions of people around them, such as joy and excitement or pain and sadness. It was already mentioned that they are indifferent towards praises or criticisms, and they can hardly understand whether someone likes them or hates them. But interestingly, schizoids do identify an offense, but they do not react emotionally. From my observations, they either ignore their offender and do not give a second about it, or they come back with a witty reply, and then again, forget about it.

Due to being pedantic and lacking empathy, schizoids are having a hard time in convincing and persuading others. Moving mountains with a speech is a trait not possessed by schizoids. This should not come up as a surprise because if you want to convince or persuade someone to a certain point, you need to emphasize with their thoughts and feelings. This way, you will get a better understanding of where a person is coming from. Furthermore, you need to ensure that you do not focus on unnecessary repetitions and corrections, as this will annoy the opposite side. It will achieve nothing but damage your influence.

Interestingly, schizoids are aware that they are introverted and lonely and face difficulties in establishing contact with people. Schizoids are also knowledgeable of the fact that they lack understanding and compassion towards others. Like hyperthymics, they are not suited for sharing the sorrow of their friends and family members.

Thought Process

Schizoids prefer living in their own world, and they love following and researching any area that interests them. They are usually inclined towards theoretical research and calculations. While analyzing the lives of some scientists, you can observe that these people care purely about their area with no regard to the pleasures of life.

Let me give some examples. Two globally renowned mathematicians, Andrew Wiles and Grigorii Perelman, are members of the schizoid psychotype. Wiles locked up himself for six years to prove Fermat's last theorem. When he presented his proof, it was shown that there was a flaw in it. He then locked himself for additional two years and came up with a robust proof.

What concerns Perelman is that he solved a millennium problem (problems in mathematics so advanced that if you solve or proof them, you will be rewarded with $1 million by Clay Mathematics Institute). Perelman proved Poincare's conjecture, but when rewarded the prize, he declined it. Also, to this day, he lives with his mother (he is 55 years old).

Schizoids

Here is the photo of famous Grigorii Perelman:

Even from his photo, it is widely visible that he is a schizoid. Not only his hair but also his beard and eyebrows are messy. His cloths are old and out of order. Note that he is also an extreme introvert who escapes from any form of social interaction.

Schizoids often drift off when someone is speaking to them. While communicating with a schizoid, it is very common that they will stop listening and start to think about something different. It is hard for these people to concentrate on what others are saying. I think the reason is that they find "us" boring. They have their own reality and truths, and they won't be interested in listening to us. However, schizoids love convincing others to their own point of view, so they will gladly talk for hours trying to convince you otherwise or to prove you wrong.

Histrionics and hyperthymics have superficial reactions to events around them, narcissistics and epileptoids have adequate reactions, while schizoids do not react. This is because of the lag in their nervous systems. It takes them a good amount of time to try and understand what happened. It takes even more time for them to understand what the most efficient reaction would be. Therefore, schizoids miss a lot of opportunities in life. You might not believe me, but I am a genetic schizoid. When I was in school, I did not have control over this field. Hence, I did not have complete command over my behavior and mind. Once my teacher told me that *"Salim, you are a smart guy, but it seems that you start the life 5 seconds later".*

Schizoids are not pragmatic; they dwell in theory and thoughts. What is more, they question the value of practice. Schizoids make up the vast majority of academics. They arrive at such scientific and theoretical developments that are hardly understood or applicable most of the time. However, it is likely that their findings will be useful sometime in the future. Though, I do not think schizoids were motivated by their findings to be applicable in any industry. It is also likely that they were not aware of what kind of developments would arise from their findings while coming up with them in the first place.

I want to give a real-life example of this. A prominent 20th century English mathematician, Godfrey Harold Hardy, developed an extensive amount of developments in number theory and mathematical analysis. Hardy is usually known by those outside the field of mathematics for his 1940 essay *"A Mathematician's Apology"*, often considered one of the best insights into the mind of a working mathematician.

What do you think was the thesis of this book? Hardy (a typical schizoid) offers a defense of his pursuit of pure mathematics in the sense of a formal justification that mathematics has a value independent of possible applications.

This part of the book is interesting:

"I have never done anything 'useful'. No discovery of mine has made or is likely to make, directly or indirectly, for good or ill, the least difference to the world's amenity. Judged by all practical standards, the value of my mathematical life is nil, and outside mathematics, it is trivial anyhow"

Today, Harold Hardy's developments are widely used in cryptography, space research, computer algorithms, and so on. However, these mathematical developments did not seem to have practical value back then. Yet, Hardy notes that the pursuit of pure mathematics not because of its applicability, but its truth:

"Pure mathematics, on the other hand, seems to be a rock on which all idealism founders: 317 is a prime, not because we think so, or because our minds are shaped in one way rather than another, but because it is, because mathematical reality is built that way."

So, for schizoids, the applications and benefits of their work are not important – they would use all their resources, including money, time, and effort, to pursue their interests, and any interference with their freedom of pursuit would irritate them. I would suggest you watch the 2015 movie *"The man who knew infinity"*. There, you can meet the globally renowned mathematician Srinivasa Ramanujan and Harold Godfrey Hardy.

While communicating with them, schizoids might interrupt you and change the topic towards the thoughts they had while they stopped listening. For this reason, they become unbearable sometimes. Therefore, dear reader, note this when communicating with schizoids. Do not take it personally when they act as such; however, do not let them get used to this either.

For example, if this is a one-time communication with a schizoid, there is no need to react. But if this is a schizoid that you will continuously interact with, try to redirect their focus back. For instance, you can use the following sentence *"an interesting thought but let us get back to what we were discussing earlier"*.

Because schizoids love their independence, a strong voice tone would be more convincing. Otherwise, schizoids will continue with what they want. If they are permitted to select the subject of debate, then they would choose whatever fits them best with total disregard towards what you want to talk about.

Influencing and Manipulating Schizoids

What are the best ways to influence schizoids? Firstly, do not expect these people to show you kindness, care, or thoughtfulness, since they live in their realm and can hardly feel the emotionality of other people. This way, you will not be developing such expectations that will put pressure on your relationship.

Secondly, do not judge or criticise them at all. Schizoids are aware that they have unusual thoughts and behaviors, and some of them develop certain insecurities due to this. Trust me, you would not be the first to judge their attitude. Every schizoid has been judged for his unusualness at least multiple times in his life. Therefore, if you try to understand them, which might be difficult, then you will get along well.

Thirdly, show care, love, and kindness towards schizoids. If the accentuation of the character is not so extreme that it resembles the traits of mental or personal disorders, then schizoids will get attached to you for being kind to them. Think of it this way. Schizoids are not the most welcomed to social gatherings or peer groups. They are always left outside looking in. Since teenage years, schizoids start suffering from loneliness, inability to communicate with others and find it almost impossible to have a friend with whom they are "best buddies". Unsuccessful attempts in establishing friendships lead schizoids to become more sensitive towards care. As such, when you approach them with a positive attitude, they will be influenced by the *scarcity*. Since it is not often for a schizoid to have the attention and care of others, he will be affected by your approach. Simply, you are giving him something that he rarely gets.

Also, there is an *element of surprise* here. As stated previously, schizoids understand that they have hardships in communicating with others, and they rarely develop friendships. After some point, they hardly expect that they will meet someone who would want to befriend them. Therefore, when you approach them in a friendly manner, they will be hit by the element of surprise, another tool of influence.

Finally, there is the *contrast principle*. If you spend quality time with a schizoid, you will naturally influence him through the contrast principle because in the case where you did not spend your time with him, he would most likely spend his time alone (as schizoids do not have many friends). And he is aware of this. He knows what his plans were going to be if he was not with you. As such, he will value the time you two have spent together a lot more than you would. This would further influence the schizoid to develop an intimate and loyal relationship with you.

Conclusion

Schizoids are distinguished through their unique, eccentric, unusual, and creative views and attitudes towards life. They have a low degree of conformity and enjoy approaching everything independently. Living a free life is crucial for them. Because these people lack intuition, they also lack a sense of empathy. They suffer a lot in relationships where their friends and partners demand admiration, care, and sympathy.

Psychotypes

In this chapter, I have not described the psychopathological cases that resemble schizoids since the literature on this topic is very broad. However, if you have the time, I suggest you to research the schizoid and schizotypal personality disorders.

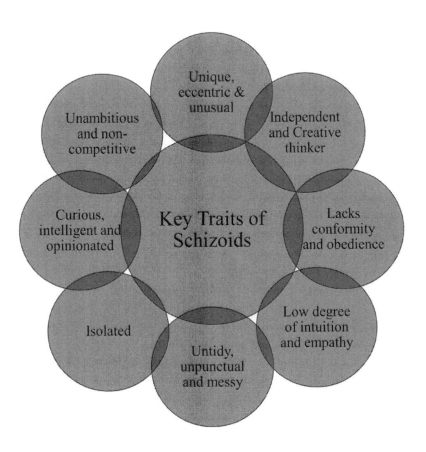

7

Narcissistics & Fanatics

"Be practical as well as generous in your ideals. Keep your eyes on the stars, but remember to keep your feet on the ground"

(Theodore Roosevelt)

We have finally arrived at the most interesting psychotypes – narcissistics and fanatics. These two psychotypes have a lot in common, but they also have certain differences. Usually, when the traits of narcissistic psychotype strengthen to a considerable degree, the person involved develops the fanatic psychotype. Developing this psychotype can also be the result of forming a huge level of resilience and strength, usually through undergoing the challenging journeys of life. As such, **no person can possess a fanatic psychotype from birth.**

This chapter is devoted to narcissistics, but we will study them simultaneously with fanatics since these two psychotypes have a lot in common. For example, both fanatics and narcissistics are target-driven. The next section covers this personality trait. I will tell you how well both fanatics and narcissistics possess this trait and how it differs among them. For instance, fanatics would cause discomfort to others in order to reach their goals but narcissistics would not.

The word *"fanatic"* comes from the Latin word *"fanaticus"*, which means *"of a temple, inspired by a god"*. Fanatics have an obsessive enthusiasm in the pursuit of their cause or objective. And they do so without any self-criticism or doubt. These people are zealous. They have a fanatical devotion to their own beliefs. I use the term *"fanatic psychotype"* to describe people who are extremely committed, devoted and fight tooth and nail for their cause. They believe that their aims and targets are divine. By achieving their cause, they believe they will benefit the many.

The hallmark of any fanatic is that they can sacrifice themselves or others to achieve their cause. They like to think that the needs of many outweigh the needs of a few. However, narcissistics do not have such perceptions. Narcissistics do not feel like it is their right or duty to make decisions that will affect others, at least without their consent. And this is the key contrast between fanatics and narcissistics that will become apparent as you study along with this chapter. Having said this, let us begin by studying narcissistics.

Narcissistics vs. Narcissists

The term "narcissistic" comes from Greek mythology, where a man called Narcissus sees his own reflection in the water and falls in love with himself. I am aware of how society perceives narcissism – negatively! We do not like pompous, arrogant, grandiose, and self-absorbed humans. We characterise such people as narcissists. However, the public knowledge of narcissism is very limited since most of us believe that narcissism is bad. But that is not the case. For me, narcissism is like a valuable poison, very healthy, but only when consumed in small doses.

I need you to start on the right foot with these people, so let us begin by comparing the narcissistic psychotype with the narcissistic personality disorder (NPD). The narcissists that you know of and despise are the people with NPD. These people are the ones who lack empathy, crave attention and admiration at extreme levels, and have an unrealistic sense of self-superiority (grandiosity). These people are not self-confident because they have a fragile ego, are full of insecurities, and cannot bear criticisms. People with the NPD seek power in order to be able to validate their grandiosity. But the way they do it is by using that power to belittle others. They have a strong desire to feel superior around people. For this reason, if they have reached any power, they are inclined to use it to abuse and control others. By diminishing people around, narcissists feel supreme.

The members of the narcissistic psychotype, however, are different. We call these people as healthy narcissists. I will refer to these people (to members of the narcissistic psychotype) simply as *"narcissistics"* and will refer to people with the NPD as *"narcissists"*. I know this might be a bit confusing, but for the lack of a better word, treat the narcissists as people with the personality disorder, and narcissistics as people with the psychotype.

Now, narcissistics do not lack empathy; in fact, they are considerate of others. It is true that they possess strong self-confidence, but they are neither delusional nor grandiose. They try to manifest their self-confidence through their talents, achievements, status, and personality. As such, they have high expectations of themselves, which is an admirable trait. (But on the negative note, when narcissistics are belittled, they get offensive). Unlike narcissists, these people have strong self-confidence; that is to say, they neither have a fragile ego nor plenty of insecurities.

Furthermore, since the self-concept of narcissistics is based on the actual reality (where the self-concept is a belief system or collection of beliefs about oneself), they can endure criticisms and reflect on themselves.

Moreover, members of the narcissistic psychotype have a strong nervous system, which further increases their endurance towards criticisms, while narcissists have a weak nervous system. Hence, criticisms affect their fragile ego. In this way, histrionics and narcissists are similar, i.e., neither of them can bear criticisms due to having a fragile ego.

As a matter of fact, histrionics are often confused with narcissists due to abundant similarities between these people. But as you will study soon, there are also many differences between these two. After completing this section, you will be able to distinguish them with an ease.

Members of the narcissistic psychotype are people who possess strong inner power and have considerable leadership qualities.

They have high expectations of themselves, and they do their best to achieve their goals. These people have a considerable amount of resilience to pursue their ideals. Note that fanatics are more resilient and driven when it comes to achieving their goals since they can sacrifice their own comfort, and if necessary, the comfort of other people as well.

Narcissistics are self-confident, self-aware, highly competitive, ambitious, and talented in leadership. They live with principles, and they defend them no matter what. On the other hand, narcissists have weak inner power, and their leadership is superficial and ineffective, just like with the members of histrionic psychotype. By trying to maximize their own self-benefit, these people can be exploitative and manipulative.

Moreover, narcissists may trade their principles and moral values in order to achieve something. Also, they get easily bored with their goals and targets. This distinguishes them from narcissistics since the members of this psychotype are obstinate and stubborn in achieving their goals.

I believe this level of comparison is sufficient in order for you to start learning about the narcissistic psychotype without any prejudice or bias. The table below summarizes the information I have presented and compares narcissistics with the narcissists:

Character Trait	Narcissistic (character)	Narcissist (disorder)
Self-confidence	Possesses strong self-confidence, which is manifested by the reality	Grandiose and Delusional. Unrealistic sense of self-superiority
Relationships	Believes in cooperation and has the willingness to reward and motivate people	Exploitative and Manipulative
Conscience	Has a respectable degree of empathy and is respectful of others' values and beliefs	Low level of empathy. Motto: ends always justify the means
Approach to Power	Views power only as a tool to reach his goals. Does not care about being viewed as powerful	Desires to reach power at all costs. Tendency to show-off his power
Values and Principles	Never compromises his moral values, beliefs or principles, regardless of the benefit	Sacrifices his values and principles in pursuit of self-benefit
Goals and Aims	Stubborn and persistent in his goals, regardless of the discomfort they may cause	Has a superficial attitude towards his goals. Easily bored and does not endure discomfort
Existence of Trauma	No related trauma	Possibility of trauma, probably from childhood

Inner Power and Leadership

Narcissistics have strong inner power, leading them to be skilfully competent, multidimensionally progressive, persistent in achieving goals, and having a disciplined mind. They can put in the necessary time and effort to hit their targets without falling into the temptation of giving up. Nonetheless, these traits are far stronger in fanatics since their perspectives are wide and goals are global. They want to contribute to the world, challenge the status quo and make a difference. This is one way how you can differentiate a fanatic from a narcissistic.

One similarity between a narcissistic and fanatic is that their lives are built on ideals and principles. However, fanatics are willing to endure high degrees of discomfort in order to reach their ideals, and even if their ideals could require causing discomfort to others, they would proceed with it. Unlike them, narcissistics are not driven enough to endure huge levels of discomfort or cause discomfort to others to pursue their goals. To give an example, if reaching his goal requires the fanatic to put someone's life in danger, he will proceed with it, though the same is not true for the narcissistics.

Of course, not all fanatics are exposed to situations where they need to cause discomfort to others in order to achieve their goals. As a result, they would not be judged as ruthless, emotionless and unempathetic. Remember, fanatics have strong principles and moral values. Therefore, when chasing their goals, they will always seek solutions that would not be damaging to anyone or be as least damaging as possible. Note that some fanatics have wide-scaled goals from which they aim to contribute to the well-being of an entire society. This trait is further strengthened when a fanatic has emotive tendencies or has branched with the emotive psychotype.

For example, Nelson Mandela and Mahatma Gandhi were both emotive fanatics. These people have their names written in the golden pages of history for overcoming the discrimination towards their culture and serving an enormous purpose. And their methods were spectacular. For instance, Gandhi led his people to success without employing violence against colonists. Meanwhile, Mandela did not discriminate against the apartheid supporters after becoming the president, and he tried to create a nation where all people could live together safely. There is even a movie on this topic called "Invictus", where Nelson Mandel is portrayed by Morgan Freeman. I would suggest you watch that movie so you can become familiar with such fanatics.

I would like to give a fictional example of a narcissistic as well. Let us take *"Jessica Pearson"* from the T.V. series "Suits". She was the head of a law firm in Manhattan. I really enjoyed how producers built her character as a pure narcissistic. She is self-confident as extremely competent and knowledgeable in her field of expertise. Narcissistics, like epileptoids, are extremely pragmatic and are highly skilled in applying their knowledge in practice. Also, Jessica Pearson is someone with strong ambition, leadership and influence – some of the key traits of the narcissistic psychotype.

External Appearance

These people look calm, confident, and sometimes severe, just like epileptoids. Narcissistics prefer strong (but not extravagant) styles when dressing (pay attention to the appearance of Jessica Pearson). The appearance of narcissistics and fanatics creates a rigid, serious, and strict impression on people. Their glowing enthusiasm, ambitiousness, competence, and natural leadership create such an aura that attracts people towards them.

Narcissistics and fanatics restore their energy by reminding themselves of their targets. That is why they can work late hours to become successful, though this trait is observed stronger in fanatics. After careful consideration, I can say that part of their success is due to their stable nature. This is a trait they share with epileptoids since all three psychotypes have a gradual nervous system. For example, a hyperthymic who has a fast nervous system reaches success by spending his energy on everything that excites him. Meanwhile, narcissistics and fanatics focus their energy only on the matters which serve their targets.

The primary emotions and thoughts of narcissistics and fanatics consist of the following:

- *Observing*: Similar to epileptoids, fanatics and narcissistics carefully observe their surroundings.

- *Seriousness and rigidity*: These people do not rush to speak their minds. They patiently wait for the right time to express their ideas. Also, it is hard to disorient them. If a fanatic or a narcissistic wants to talk about a specific topic, then regardless of your several attempts to change the conversation, they will remain focused and bring you back to the previous topic.

- *Contempt*: One of the fundamental emotions of narcissistics and fanatics. A contempt is such an emotion where you regard the individual in front of you as inferior. Fanatics and narcissistics use this emotion frequently towards people who are standing against their values, morals, beliefs, goals, and targets.

Narcissistics and fanatics constantly try to seem authoritative in society. They mask their feelings if they are having troubles in their personal life. When their friends or relatives die, they remain cold-blooded in front of those who express their condolences. It is not possible to see these people cry. Furthermore, predicting the mimicries of narcissistics and fanatics is a fool's errand because these people manage their emotions perfectly.

Take an epileptoid, for example. Epileptoids cannot hide their feelings of anger or dysphoria since they explode after one point. However, fanatics and narcissistics hide such emotions. The most negative emotion that these people might show to others is contempt. Nonetheless, this applies more to fanatics than narcissistics because after some accumulation of negative feelings, narcissistics may explode the way epileptoids do. But indeed, the inner power of narcissistics is much higher due to their strong nervous system. Hence, they can endure a lot more negative provocations than epileptoids.

Narcissistics and fanatics have natural leadership behaviors and gestures. When using motivating gestures in a conversation, they express serious and regulated mimics. These people can move the mountains with their words – a quality from their leadership. Because of their particular voice tone, gestures, and self-confidence, people trust them. We can usually see these behaviors in the speech of presidents in front of crowds. These people have such an aura that attracts and persuades people in their goals.

Thought Process

Both narcissistics and fanatics have a strong and gradual nervous system. Do you remember the personality traits arising from having a gradual nervous system? Let us go over them briefly. To begin with, such people do not rush in making judgements and decisions; instead, they take enough time to think things through. Being patient and observant are among common character traits of people with a gradual nervous system. In addition, these people are analytical and enjoy establishing their ideas on valid arguments. Similarly, they are detail-oriented.

Psychotypes

There are three psychotypes that have a gradual nervous system: epileptoids, narcissistics, and fanatics. The members of these psychotypes gather details, analytically process them and then deduce arguments. Only after having enough arguments, they reach a conclusion. Therefore, it is hard to prove these people wrong.

Nonetheless, it is easier to convince narcissistics and fanatics to a contrary opinion compared to epileptoids. This is because epileptoids are extremely stubborn, i.e., they get angry and stubbornly resist when people disagree with them or hold contrary views. Narcissistics and fanatics, on the other hand, listen to others' ideas, and if they genuinely think they have miscalculated something, they adjust their beliefs. Epileptoids, though, are obstinate in their beliefs and will hardly ever change.

Similar to epileptoids, both narcissistics and fanatics get pay attention to everything that evolves around them. But unlike epileptoids, these people do not dwell too much on details. Do not got me wrong, narcissistics and fanatics want to maintain order and keep things under control. After all, these people enjoy being in charge. But they do not spread themselves too thin. They would rather assign the tasks with a lot of boring details to either hypothymics or epileptoids rather than "wasting" their time on it. Exactly. These people think that a work with a lot of details, such as filling out a paperwork, is below them. Instead, they should be handling the important managerial stuff, such as assigning and distributing tasks, deciding on the monetary spending of the firm, and so on.

The high level of mental capacity, resilience, and endurance arising from having a strong nervous system allow these people to manage an exhausting degree of mental pressure without getting overwhelmed. For this reason, these people do not get irritated when their ideas are challenged and are capable of adjusting their beliefs if necessary.

Epileptoids, on the other hand, are different in this regard. For instance, an epileptoid, who reached a certain conclusion after putting an immense amount of mental work becomes stubborn on his point of view, will relentlessly protect it and will be irritated if someone challenges his perspective. This is because agreeing to a contrary view would mean to have miscalculated something – there is something he has not been aware of!

This idea is terrifying for epileptoids as these people cannot ignore anything. If they have miscalculated something, then they will research it. And this, in turn, means putting in an extra degree of mental effort. As these people have a weak nervous system, they do not want to overwhelm themselves further with extra research. Instead of undergoing an additional degree of discomfort, it is better for them to stubbornly resist others and ignore their contrary perspectives at all costs, even if it means living in denial, even if it means not improving any further. But does this fact about epileptoids surprise us? Indeed not. Recall that inertia is one of the core personality traits of epileptoids.

Narcissistics and fanatics are rational. They refrain from acting emotionally. This comes from having a strong nervous system. These people always choose to act reasonably and rationally. They make their decisions according to their logic, opinion, and principles. Nonetheless, they still listen to other people in order to get their perspectives as well.

I have a dear friend whose genetic psychotype is a schizoid but has branched into a narcissistic character, classifying him as a narcissistic schizoid. Whenever his friends end up in disagreements, they always approach him. Because my friend approaches everything logically with no regard to emotionality, people listen to him carefully and trust his judgements. Some individuals, on the other hand, are unable to get along with him because he is very argumentative and enjoys using his abilities to play with others (this trait comes from being a schizoid).

The reason why we can get along is that both of us love debating. He finds it a hobby while I find it a practice to polish my influence skills. We both listen to one another's ideas carefully and almost never reach a consensus. However, we both enjoy it and find it productive. Both of us listen to one another attentively and by doing so, we improve our mental capacity.

This trait is at the core of what fanatics and narcissistics do — they want to improve their mental capacity to move towards their targets. They want to know and remember such information which is accurate and comprehensive, even if it comes from others. This is a key reason why these people are not stubborn in their ideas. Although a strong nervous system allows them to adjust their belief systems, personal development is what motivates them to do so.

There are several benefits of having a strong nervous system, such as a high degree of self-esteem, attention, mental capacity, resilience, and being well in a crisis. Also, having a strong nervous system would mean that you are not a touchy person. It is hard to offend such people. Narcissistics and fanatics possess all of these traits. For instance, if you try to provoke someone with a strong nervous system, let us say by downgrading their achievements, then it is very likely that they will either not react to it or react humorously by saying something like "*eh eh eh, of course ...*". That is to say, in situations where others try to provoke them, fanatics and narcissistics will neither react negatively nor will they show any emotion towards it. There are three reasons behind this.

Firstly, people with a strong nervous system usually have a high degree of self-esteem, i.e., they are highly self-aware and comfortable with themselves. For this reason, whether you try to flatter or belittle these people, it is not going to work. Secondly, narcissistics and fanatics ignore those people who try to offend them. Because members of these psychotypes have a considerable degree of status, they do not fight people who are disrespectful in nature. By ignoring such people, fanatics and narcissistics are actually saying that *"you are not someone worth my while"*.

Now, the final reason people with fanatic or narcissistic psychotype do not react towards people who try to offend them is that they do not want to give pleasure or satisfaction to those people.

Fanatics and Narcissistics

These people are aware that their offenders are trying to get under their skin. This is their target. Being target-driven themselves, fanatics and narcissistics understand this naturally. Hence, they ensure that their offenders do not get what they want by reacting negatively or aggressively, as epileptoids do.

It was already mentioned that the members of narcissistic and fanatic psychotype are target-driven. These people have wide-scaled thoughts, and they keep up with the global developments. It is often observed that these people are highly familiar with developments in technology and politics. They try to stay ahead of things and cope with it by having daily routines, such as listening to morning and evening news. They have a systematic and structural approach towards their goals and ambitions.

This should not come up as a surprise since being systematic and structural is a trait arising from having a gradual nervous system, as you have studied in epileptoids. But there is one nuance that you should be aware of. For epileptoids, the motive behind being systematic and structural lies in the fact that it helps them to avoid getting exhausted or overwhelmed. For fanatics and narcissistics, it helps in reaching their goals and targets.

What combines epileptoids, narcissistics, fanatics, and even rhapsodics is that all the members of these psychotypes are highly doubtful. But again, there are differences in motives behind this personality trait. For epileptoids, the motive is ensuring their safety and stability. These people are doubtful and sceptical of others; hence, they keep their distance from others. Also, people usually lack personal control with those they feel close to.

Epileptoids do not like such behaviors – they always want others to have personal control. Otherwise, epileptoids get to a dysphoric state and later explode. For rhapsodics, being doubtful and cautious arises due to their extreme risk-averse nature. It is for this reason that rhapsodics are known as "psychasthenics". Psychasthenia is a neurotic state defined by irrational fears, phobias, obsessions, etc.

You would not believe it, but I have a rhapsodic friend who once spent his whole day with me in order to ensure that nothing bad happens to me. He acted as such because he had a nightmare in which I ended up being dead. Indeed, his fear was irrational since life is not predictable based on our dreams. Yet, he annoyed me so much that I was almost going to fulfil his dream by throwing myself out of a window.

Now, narcissistics and fanatics, having a strong emotional intelligence, enjoy keeping people at a certain distance. There are a few reasons behind this, with two being the same as for epileptoids. First and foremost, these people want to protect their status. Therefore, they always keep a certain distance from people. Secondly, these people do not like getting emotionally attached to others since it might cloud their judgement.

Thirdly, keeping distance from people ensures that others do not act uncontrollably or hysterically towards them. Finally, these people are sceptical and doubtful of others. It is highly difficult for them to trust someone completely since they do not want to do it in the first place. From the T.V. series "Valley of the Wolves", the character "Mehmet Karahanli", a typical fanatic, has stated once that: *"30 years is enough of a time to know someone, but not enough to trust"*.

Fanatics and narcissistics keep their speeches under control. They do not rush in making their points; instead, they wait for the appropriate moment. These people express their thoughts succinctly but still comprehensively. It is hard to disorient these people from the topics that they want to talk about.

Assume they start talking to you about a specific topic, let's say about the importance of teamwork in a corporate environment. Assume at one point you deviate from the core topic of debate and start talking about how you have developed your teamwork skills. When this happens, narcissistics or fanatics will interrupt you at an appropriate moment and redirect you back to the main point. They may do so by saying something like:

"Interesting, thanks for sharing it. But if we shall return to the importance of teamwork in ..."

Fanatics

In the previous chapters, we learnt what happens to histrionics and epileptoids when their characters accentuate pathologically, resulting in HPD and OCPD, respectively (typically with antisocial elements in epileptoids). Of course, it does not mean that if you are an individual with the HPD, then you had a histrionic character which extremely accentuated. The pathological accentuation of character may cause the personality disorder, but as was stated previously, not all personality disorders are caused by the pathological accentuation.

The following conditions, for instance, are among frequent causes of certain personality disorders:

1) Diseases (brain injuries, infections, intoxication, psychotraumas, and so on)

2) Congenital neural system inferiority due to heredity, birth injury, etc.

3) Social reasons (being a victim of bullying, treason, unfaithfulness, etc.)

Interestingly, there is not anything like *"pathological accentuation of the narcissistic psychotype"* simply because narcissistic psychotype cannot accentuate pathologically. In addition, accentuation of this psychotype can never lead to the NPD. The narcissistic personality disorder has its own causes. But does it mean that the narcissistic psychotype cannot accentuate to an extreme level? It can, and it does! But it does not lead to a personality disorder. It leads to another psychotype – the fanatic psychotype.

The fanatic psychotype is a much stronger version of the narcissistic psychotype. These people believe that needs of many outweigh the needs of a few, and for this reason, unlike the narcissistic psychotype, they can and will cause discomfort to others if it serves the greater good. Interestingly, fanatics assume the right to decide those needs of many, even though public opinion might not be on their side.

This is because fanatics are zealous and are obsessively enthusiastic about their beliefs. They lack criticism and doubt towards their ideas. They do not question if they are wrong. They believe they are right, no matter what. If the cause that a fanatic fights for is universally beneficial and agreed upon by all, then there is no reason for concern. Examples include Gandhi and Mandela. But if not, then it might be damaging to others.

I would like to give a fictional example of this. I think all of you have watched *"Avengers: Infinity War"*. Remember the character, *"Thanos"*. He decided, on his own, that the universe would suffer due to overpopulation, based on what happened on his own planet. Afterward, he aimed to save the whole universe from potential extinction, and to achieve this, he has decided to diminish half of the population through genocide. As you can imagine, no one would agree to this. But it does not matter for fanatics. They do not care about the thoughts and opinions of others. Their own opinions is all that matters to them. They think they have the right to do what they feel is right, even if it means causing great suffering to many others. To put it another way, fanatics feel that ends justify the means. They fight for their cause, no matter what.

Fanatics are willing to sacrifice everything in the path of achieving their goals and ambitions. They are even capable of injuring their beloved ones. For example, in his path to get one of the infinity stones, Thanos has sacrificed his daughter, Gamora.

Nonetheless, it was an important decision that needed to be made. At the end of the movie, you can see him chatting with his daughter's childhood and getting affected when she asks him: *"at what cost"*. Whether you think his ambition was good or bad, Thanos is a character who belongs to the fanatic psychotype. These people are willing to take extreme measures in order to reach their goals and ambitions.

The members of fanatic psychotype can sacrifice their comfort for the sake of their targets. As mentioned, there are instances when they can sacrifice other people's comfort as well. Although this personality trait applies to people with the NPD as well, to identify whether the individual has the mental disorder or the fanatic psychotype, you will need to look closer at the purpose of the decision that they made. Was it due to self-serving reasons? Or was it for the greater good?

For individuals with the NPD, human morality does not play any role, and they cause discomfort to others due to being exploitative and manipulative. For these people, discomfort to others is justified if the result is self-beneficial. Nonetheless, fanatics think that ends always justify means only if these "ends", according to their own opinion, lead to a situation where the "greater good" is served.

Are there real-life examples of fanatics? Yes. Many of the world leaders belong to the fanatic psychotype.

I would like to give a historical example. If we look at World War II, the son of Joseph Stalin, Yakov Dzhugashvili, was seized by the Germans. When the Soviet army captured the Nazi general, Marshal Friedrich von Paulus, the Germans proposed an exchange: the son against the marshal. Stalin's response was: *"I do not trade a marshal for a soldier"*. After this reply, the German army killed Yakov. I would like you to think: by sacrificing his son, did Stalin have the mental disorder, or was he a member of the fanatic psychotype?

We cannot say for sure whether Stalin did or did not have a personality disorder merely from this story. However, his actions relate more to the fanatic psychotype than to some personality disorder. Think of it this way. Was Stalin's son any different from any other militant who fought day and night with the enemy, sacrificing blood, flesh, and tears? Would it be in the interest of the nation to exchange a marshal for Stalin's son?

The answer is no. Stalin's son was a mere soldier, not a military expert, and going through this exchange could have had a severe negative impact on the USSR. Stalin made that choice as the head of the USSR. He could not have made that decision as a father simply because it was the head of the USSR who could define the fate of the marshal, not a father of a mere militant.

Let's take a look at the photo of Stalin below. His external appearance radiates of a fanatic. His visage is a mix of pride and contempt. These are among the foundational emotions of fanatics. He also has a neat and tidy appearance. This is a common trait that fanatics have in common with epileptoids (and narcissistics). Nonetheless, if you look at his forehead, you can see that there is no swelling – epileptoids usually have swelled foreheads due to constantly narrowing their eyebrows from aggression. His hair is directed backward – a quality belonging mainly to fanatics. Thus, we can assert that Stalin was a fanatic based on his external appearance.

Among all psychotypes, fanatics are the best influencers. The strong inner power gives them strong confidence. They can easily use a wide range of tools to manipulate people since they observe people very attentively. They value both the positive and negative points of their opponents. This makes the debater vulnerable since the fanatic will understand his idea perfectly and will know where to strike. He may try to absurd the argumentation of his opponent and lead him to a breaking point.

There might be multiple reasons for fanatics to do this. I will just write a few:

1) By breaking the debater's argumentation, the fanatic will strengthen his status and be able to influence the wider public

2) Fanatic might want to change the point of view of the debater for his own ambitions and interests (he might need the debater to act differently)

3) Fanatic might want to break the confidence of the debater just to weaken him and regain dominance.

As you see from above, there must always be some sort of a payoff for a fanatic to engage in manipulative behavior. If a histrionic is provoking someone, the reason behind it is either to show off or break the individual's confidence and gain pleasure from it. Fanatics do not use these motives as a reason for manipulation. Indeed, any instrument from their toolkit will only be used if there is a necessity or benefit from it.

How do you think fanatics lie? Know this: fanatics are the best liars. Due to their strong and gradual nervous system, they are capable of lying systematically. They create a whole scenario with decent details and can sell them effectively to others. In fact, deception is one of the most effective manipulation techniques if you can speak with details and remember them later. Fanatics may lie to people for various reasons, but the motive behind these reasons is the same – gaining something in return or preventing something bad from happening.

Fanatics aren't the kind to flaunt their strength or seek to look powerful. These are the characteristics of narcissists. Why do you think fanatics refrain from showing their power? Well, they do that because they aim to catch their enemies off guard. Because fanatics are suspicious and distrustful, they seek to identify people who may pose a potential threat. I would like to ask you a question. If there are people who harbour bad thoughts towards you, then is it likely that they will talk about their thoughts if you are someone who looks powerful or someone who looks weak? The answer is obvious.

I already mentioned the character "Mehmet Karahanli" from the Turkish T.V. series called *"Valley of Wolves"*. In one instance, he is being advised by the head of his security that a certain individual might be your enemy, allow us to raise the security to the maximum level when he arrives to meet you. Mehmet Karahanli's response was:

> *"Why would I appear strong to my enemy? Let him see me weak, approach me carelessly so I can rip them to pieces"*

Photo of Mehmet Karahanli, from the series:

There are some last points that I would like to make before concluding the chapter. Fanatics are people that think thoroughly before speaking. Therefore, it is very difficult to learn something from them if they are unwilling to disclose it. For example, there were several allegations by the U.S. government that Russian leadership had interfered in the 2016 presidential elections.

Now, I cannot say whether it is the truth or not, but Mr. Vladimir Putin's response to those allegations was highly adequate. As a fanatic leader, he crashed all the allegations thrown at him in multiple interviews, meetings, and so on.

Since 2016, he has been actively denying any Russian interference in the U.S. elections. After a few years, he was asked by the journalist Keir Simmons if Russia would interfere in the 2020 U.S. presidential elections. The response of Mr. Putin was strong enough to end that subject:

> *"Will tell you in secret, yes! Absolutely we will be doing it. So that you guys can get totally excited over there. But do not tell anyone"*

In his response, Mr. Putin has used a manipulation technique called "absurding". In this technique, one makes his opponent believe that his arguments, questions, or statements are highly absurd. There are multiple ways in which the manipulator can achieve this. I have listed two of the ways you can use the absurding technique below:

1) ***Accepting or agreeing to a self-incriminating statement***: In this technique, the manipulator purposefully accepts or agrees to a self-incriminating statement in an amusing manner to either mock his offender or reduce the seriousness of the situation. Basically, the manipulator tells everyone that the topic is so absurd that he does not even care to take it seriously. Mr. Putin's response to Keir Simmon is an example of this technique. The effectiveness of this technique is strengthened with the element of fun.

2) ***Size Distortion***: With this technique, the manipulator either overstates or understates his opponent's arguments or statements. For example, if your teammate says, *"look, that is not the correct way of doing this"*, then you will be using the size distortion technique if you reply as: *"of course, only you know the correct way of doing things"*.

The absurding technique does not work if you use it too early in an argument, and it could backfire on you. For example, if the person in front of you is acting reasonably, then a rational and argumentative response is enough for you to achieve what you want. The technique works the best when you use it against people who have been acting stubbornly. But the technique will backfire as well if you use it too late. Suppose you have already overargued with someone on a particular topic. In that case, your use of absurd technique will be perceived as if you have lost your temper or patience, neither of which are the attributes of a person with strong inner power.

Narcissistic Personality Disorder

Now, let us talk about the personality disorder regarding narcissism. Well, as the name suggests, these people have a sense of superiority at grandiose levels, combined with extreme arrogance and pretentiousness.

Despite having a high opinion of themselves, i.e., having self-generated notions about their talents, skills, and intellect, these individuals have a fragile ego and poor self-esteem. For this reason, they want others to admire them, and they desperately need them. When they cannot see the admiration and approval of others, they get out of control.

While we are supposed to praise and admire them, they are supposed to belittle us. One way a narcissist feels grandiose is by belittling people around him. They do not like when people they work with come up with original ideas. If there is an idea that should be accepted and to be executed upon, that definitely must be the narcissist's idea.

Otherwise, we are mentally-ill ingrates who cannot see how "blessed" we are by working with that narcissist. This is how narcissists position themselves in society. We, "simpletons", have one goal in this world – to execute the orders and wishes of the narcissist. And we must do so while simultaneously expressing our gratitude to them, for we have been "lucky" to be taking part in building their legacy.

As you can see from these traits, narcissists are very different when compared to narcissistics or fanatics. The members of these psychotypes do not belittle people around them as such. Although they can have a feeling of self-superiority, it is justifiable due to two reasons. First, they never tell or express their superiority towards others. They find such behavior stupid. Second, they feel superior only if their talents, ambitions, ideals and achievements manifest them.

Narcissists are so egocentric that they are willing to sacrifice other people's comfort, resources, desires, and property for their own gains. Relationships with these people may easily become toxic. Jealousy and distrust towards their partners are among their main qualities. This is due to their low self-confidence and self-esteem.

Also, they project their own lack of moral values onto their partners. For example, narcissists are extremely distrustful towards their partners because they are unfaithful themselves. Because they may have a romantic or sexual relationship with someone else, they start fearing that so can their partner. Such projection leads to an extreme amount of interrogation in the relationship.

I've always thought narcissists were delusional, and there are many reasons for this. An overwhelming feeling of grandiosity and self-superiority does, in fact, partly explain this. However, what strikes me the most is how these people rationalize their egoistic desires in order to justify their bad behavior or to persuade others to do what they want.

Fanatics and Narcissistics

Once I watched an interrogation of a narcissist who had been caught in a serious crime. When the interrogation started, he denied any involvement in the crime and called his interrogators "idiots" for bringing in the wrong guy. He then pursued to threatening them – that he will make them pay the moment they realize they have got the wrong guy.

Several threats, such as suing, complaining to the ministry of internal affairs, even to "Human Rights Watch". In the end, they showed him the videotape that located him at the scene of the crime committing that very crime of which he was accused. Afterward, he started to explain why he committed that crime and that he was right in doing so. He attempted to totally rationalise his wrongdoings and tried to convince people in the room that they would be wrong to prosecute him for that crime.

So, even if you catch narcissists dead to rights, they will not surrender easily as they will rationalise their actions ad nauseam. They will never give the reaction you expect; quite the contrary, they will react in a dismissive and condescending manner.

All in all, narcissism is a personality disorder, and it would be my personal suggestion to avoid narcissists at all costs. Giving them a piece of your own mind will never lead to anything good.

I would like to conclude this part by providing the mnemonic of Pinkofsky for narcissistic personality disorder. He has used the term "S P E E E C I A L" with three E's.

S	Special: believes he is special and unique
P	Preoccupied with fantasies of unlimited success, power, brilliance and so on
E	Envious: is envious of others and believes that others are envious of him
E	Entitled
E	Excess admiration required
C	Conceited: grandiose sense of self-importance
I	Interpersonal exploitation
A	Arrogant and haughty
L	Lacks empathy

Conclusion

In this chapter, you learned about narcissistics and fanatics. The main character traits of these psychotypes include high inner power, resilience, patience, analysis, leadership, and being influential. These people, like epileptoids, burden themselves as well. But due to having a strong nervous system, they do not get overwhelmed. You also discovered that the fanatic psychotype could not be acquired by a genetic or biogenetic component. It can be acquired either through strengthening of the narcissistic traits or growing from the challenging life experiences.

Fanatics and narcissistics are not frequented often, but if you ever do meet these people, it is important you can influence and establish a strong relationship with them. Such people are usually frequented in positions of influence and status, such as in high levels of the political or corporate ladder. The most important thing you have to keep in mind is not to reveal your cards to them. Fanatics and narcissistics will leverage your weaknesses to negotiate with you. For example, if you are being interviewed by a fanatic and you tell him that you want to change your job because you are being treated unfairly, then he will use this to negotiate on your salary or title.

One of the good ways to cooperate with these people is to show them how you can contribute towards their targets. Do not forget; these people are target-driven; hence, they want to surround themselves with people who can help them in achieving their goals. If you have strong qualities and skills that you can bring to the table, then talk about them – do not be shy. Be self-confident, but not arrogant. Focus on outcomes: if you can persuade a narcissistic or fanatic about the virtues of a project, he will commit to it. Their tenacity aids them in putting in the time and effort necessary to attain their objectives. They are more inclined to believe in your opinions if you back them up with quotations from influential and well-known individuals.

8

Emotives

"The best and most beautiful things in the world cannot be seen or even touched. They must be felt with the heart"

(Hellen Keller)

Also known as sensitives, the members of emotive psychotype, as their names suggest, are very sensitive and emotional people. They set up their life based on harmony, mutual love, and empathy towards others. Not only do they set high moral standards upon themselves, but they also demand others to approach them with a high degree of morality. They do not tolerate negativity and escape such situations. The main character traits of emotives include excessive sensitivity towards their environment, and a kind and attentive attitude towards people. Unlike schizoids, the members of this psychotype have a strong sense of intuition, hence, are very empathetic and careful towards the reactions of others.

Emotives are dependable and loyal. Although members of this psychotype have a healthy degree of altruism and selflessness, these traits can get out of proportion. They can become self-damaging given that emotives are naïve in nature. Their ill-natured friends exploit this trait, e.g., asking for money through pretending that they are in urgent need. Emotives usually love listening to people with great pleasure during conversations. These people would give you advice for solving your problem and support you until you overcome it.

In this chapter, you will examine the behavior of emotives. I believe it will be an extremely easy read since it is the shortest chapter in the book. Much to my regret, it is not frequent to meet emotives as they are a dying race in an era of increasing individualism and narcissism. Nonetheless, this psychotype constitutes one of the main forms of character that humans may possess and, therefore, important to be knowledgeable of.

Thought Process

Emotives have a weak and slow nervous system. We have previously studied various forms of nervous systems of psychotypes, such as fast and weak (histrionics), gradual and weak (epileptoids), strong and fast (hyperthymics), and strong and gradual (narcissistics and fanatics). Let us now study character traits from a slow and weak nervous system.

Slow Nervous System: Emotives lack rational traits. While narcissistics and epileptoids' possession of a gradual nervous system makes them analytical and rational, emotive's slow nervous system inhibits the level of his analysis. It would take a lot of time for such people to come up with an effective solution to a problem. This leads them to appear as irrational and selfless as well.

The motivations of most people in helping others are self-interested. For instance, we help others to receive their approval, admiration, trust and so on. We might even do so to reap some future benefits. However, emotives help others in a selfless manner. The only enjoyment they get from helping others is the pleasure of seeing it.

Weak Nervous System: Their weak nervous system attacks their resilience directly. For example, emotives feel uncomfortable in large public gatherings. This is because large public gatherings are such environments where many people are talking simultaneously.

Due to having a weak nervous system, emotives get overwhelmed. Hence, they do not enjoy an environment where many things co-occur. This is what epileptoids have in common with emotives, as the former also has a weak nervous system. But you may ask, why do histrionics, who also have a weak nervous system, enjoy large public crowds? Given that their nervous system is weak as well, why would the members of the histrionic psychotype thrive in large public gatherings while epileptoids and emotives would want to avoid them?

The difference comes in their ambitions and goals. The large public gatherings are opportunities for histrionics to get attention. Remember, histrionics thrive for the approval and attention of others, and therefore, are exhibitionists. Environments with many people are perfect places for exhibitionist behavior. Epileptoids endure large public gatherings if the aim is to network or establish business connections, but because emotives are less likely to possess such goals and care as epileptoids, they will always try to avoid such environments.

The resilience of emotives towards stress is weak. A corporate lifestyle is likely to burn them out. They are more fit for creative areas – art, programming, music, and so on.

A weak nervous system affects emotives differently than histrionics. If a histrionic craves attention due to his weak nervous system, emotive's weak nervous system directly leads him to be selfless. Because their fortitude to stress is very low, they can easily get offended. When others propose negative thoughts and opinions, emotives struggle to let go.

This is because emotives naturally act in a friendly and helpful manner, and when subjected to negative views, they feel that they have been treated unfairly. And then they start thinking a lot about why someone would treat them unfairly. This causes a self-reinforcing cycle of anxiety and stress, i.e., the more stressed and anxious a person feels, the harder it is to let go of things. And when it gets harder to let go of things, the stronger the emotions of stress and anxiety become. Even constructive criticisms are problematic. Therefore, you have to be very polite and gentle when talking to emotives.

People with a weak nervous system are hardly oriented to the future. It is primarily the traits of people with a strong nervous system to be future-oriented, e.g., narcissistics and fanatics. These people are oriented towards the future benefits and costs of their actions. They get motivation and inspiration by visualising the profits they will reap in the time to come.

Emotives, in contrast, are oriented towards the past. What do you think are the personality traits arising from being a past-oriented individual? Firstly, these people recall their past experiences and memories frequently. These memories could be past successes, holiday trips, family gatherings, romantic relationships, and so on. Simply put, these people recall the good old times. They tend to preserve the objects that maintain those memories. For example, an emotive who has spent a vacation with her friends on an exotic island will collect some pebbles from the beach or buy a souvenir resembling the nature of that island. Furthermore, gifts with sentimental value, such as a flower, a letter, or a bracelet, will be carefully looked after.

These people also accumulate photos and videos capturing the good old times. Nostalgia is among the common traits observed in emotives. If you want to influence emotives, talk about your interesting emotional experiences from the past, such as how fun it was when you visited some place with your friends or family. Never talk about negative experiences – it will burden them.

Emotives do not focus on negative memories, such as past regrets, failures, and mistakes. They try to forget them, and they do so by recalling the good memories. This is among the crucial traits of emotives that help them to forgive their friends. For example, suppose an epileptoid gets offended by his friend. In that case, he will immediately start treating him negatively, without considering how good this person has been to him in the past or how this will damage the relationship in the future. Fanatics and narcissistics, on the other hand, will not escalate the situation if the person who offended them will be useful in the future.

Emotives, in contrast, will focus on past experiences and will be more forgiving. Although emotives are touchy, i.e., even slight criticisms can cause huge discomfort, stress, and anxiety, they tend to forgive their offenders, and they do so by recalling positive memories with that person. This is due to two reasons: firstly, forgiving releases the emotive from stress and anxiety, and secondly, emotives are friendly and caring in their nature and cannot hold a grudge towards someone for a long time. However, if an emotive concludes that her friend has been constantly unfair or rude, she will start distancing herself.

Social Relationships and External Appearance

Emotives have a greater ability to listen and affirm, greater empathy and intuitiveness, better understanding of others' wants and needs, and so on. So, it would seem that calling them "sensitives" is a better use of the word. However, the reason why I do not call "emotives" as "sensitives" is because there are two psychotypes that are highly sensitive: emotives and rhapsodics.

Emotives are mostly sensitive towards positive emotions and feelings, while rhapsodics to fear, cautiousness, and wariness. Nonetheless, emotives are vulnerable to negative emotions as well. These people tend to take things personally because they hardly project negative traits to other people. For example, if someone acts rudely towards them, then they will start thinking about what they did wrong in the first place to trigger such a negative response.

Unlike these psychotypes, histrionics never admit guilt – they always treat the opposing individual negatively for their rudeness. If you end up in a conflict with a histrionic, he will firstly act abruptly, but then forget about it very quickly and continue his life as if nothing has happened.

Do you remember the reason behind this? Because of their shallow and superficial attitude, histrionics do not dwell in thoughts and past negative experiences, which leads to a lack of self-reflection. Unlike histrionics, emotives can hardly let go of negative memories.

Similar to epileptoids, emotives thrive towards maintaining their own safety and security. These people are not inclined towards alcoholism or drug abuse. They escape friend groups involved in delinquency and risky behaviors. Since their school ages, emotives make one or two friends as they prefer spending their time only with a limited number of people that they trust. Although they usually get invited to friendly events, such as birthday parties or casual hangouts, and they indeed participate in those gatherings, emotives do not thrive towards having a large inner circle. These people are private and discreet. Moreover, they dislike uncertainty, and therefore, they reduce their social activities so that their exposure to unpredictable actions is automatically lower.

Emotives hardly smoke, drink or consume drugs. In cases of alcohol consumptions, it is often to see not a euphoric but rather a depressive reaction. This is because, under the influence, emotives experience self-inferiority, leading to an intropunitive state of mind. In these situations, crying or complaining are among the most frequent things that emotives do. While alcohol helps schizoids to reduce their psychological barrier in socialising with people, it produces the opposite effect with emotives. Under the influence, these people neither facilitate contacts nor inspire confidence (due to self-deprecation and depressiveness).

Now I would like to give a fictional example for an emotive. I believe you have all watched the movie Green Mile. The actor, Michael Clarke Duncan, who portrayed John Coffey, is a typical emotive. His main characteristics were love, kindness, harmony, desire to help people, purity, and self-sacrifice.

Conclusion

Emotives are very sensitive people; thus, try using delightful emotions when communicating with emotives. Let them take care of you because they adore looking after people. Also, pay them sincere attention and genuine love. Once, when I was having a party, one of my Russian friends hugged me in such a strong way that it strained my back muscles, and I was having minor pain. One of my emotive friends, who saw my pain, approached me and proposed teaching me some acrobatic moves to relieve my pain. Understanding that he was an emotive, I agreed, and he spent the next 15 minutes massaging me.

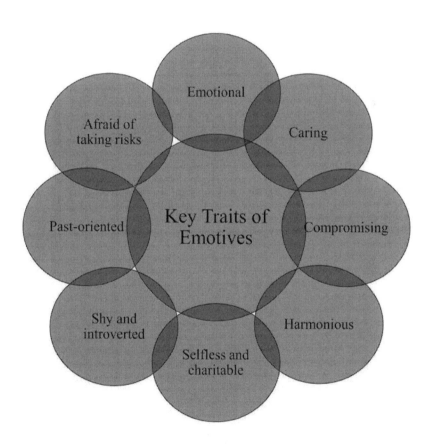

9

Rhapsodics

"When I look back on all these worries, I remember the story of the old man who said on his deathbed that he had had a lot of trouble in his life, most of which had never happened"

(Winston Churchill)

In this chapter, we will study the members of rhapsodic psychotype, or simply, rhapsodics. The ***fundamental character traits of these people are extreme lack of resilience towards stress and considerable risk-aversion.*** They cannot tolerate stressful environments and do their best to escape them. Rhapsodics are mentally overwhelmed and anxious. The weakness towards stress arises from their fast and weak nervous system. The weakness of the nervous system leads to a lack of resilience; meanwhile, having a fast nervous system results in inadequate and shallow responses when subjected to stress. Therefore, it is more efficient for these people to run away the moment they feel stressed, rather than trying to decide analytically and rationally on the correct course of action.

P. Gannushkin (1933) used the term "psychasthenic" to characterize these people, as psychasthenia is a mental state occupied with irrational fears, phobias, compulsions and obsessions. For example, rhapsodics always feel that they must do something; otherwise, things could go wrong. As such, they constantly double-check things to ensure that everything is safe and accurate.

In a professional environment, these people are grinders. They come to work earlier than everyone and do not leave until they are completely sure they have done everything required. They fear for their position at work and are afraid of losing it. The degree of self-esteem is considerably low, and they need the approval of someone of considerable degree or status. As such, rhapsodics always tend to strong romantic partners.

Many of you might have watched the series "*Suits*". The character "Louis Litt" is a genetic rhapsodic. He falls into the category of "aggressive rhapsodics", which I will talk about later. It is a type of rhapsodic whose main instincts under stress are irrational dysphoric explosions, as observed in epileptoids.

Here is the photo of "Louis Litt" from the "Suits" series:

Rhapsodics have a lot in common with epileptoids. Since these people have a considerable degree of fear, the hallmark of their personality is radiant risk-aversion and cautiousness. They plan and organize their responsibilities with great effort, and if their plans are disturbed, they start feeling stressed as they fear things could go irreversibly wrong.

As epileptoids, rhapsodics are disciplined and approach their responsibilities in a systematic way. They try insuring themselves from mistakes as much as possible. I had a rhapsodic friend back in the university. He told me that he would start preparing 3 hours in advance to avoid any possible delay whenever he had a meeting with someone. He was always the first to arrive at class.

He would arrive at the exam hall at least 2 hours before the start of the exam. When invited to college parties, he would ensure to leave at least two hours before midnight, for the night is dark and full of terrors. Or maybe he was not rhapsodic after all. Maybe he just watched "Game of Thrones" a lot of times.

But the key difference between epileptoids and rhapsodics, aggressive rhapsodics in particular, is the lower degree of self-esteem. For example, both epileptoids and aggressive rhapsodics explode at people when they are overwhelmed. But an epileptoid will keep negativity towards the person he exploded at even after he calms down. This is because he wants his current behavior to be consistent with the previous one. Also, it is almost impossible to sway them otherwise as they are very stubborn.

Epileptoids feel all right about the idea of not compromising with people. Rhapsodics, on the other hand, are not so stubborn, as they do not have a substantial degree of self-confidence, and they fear the consequences of not compromising. As such, these people may accept guilt even if they were not guilty in the first place. That is to say, rhapsodics may judge themselves intropunitively when someone lashes out on them, even if they are at right.

For instance, if you have watched "*Suits*", then you know there were several instances when the character "*Harvey Specter*" lashed out on "*Louis Litt*" in a very extreme and unfair manner. Nonetheless, Louis could not stand up against Harvey and always blamed himself due to the feelings of self-inferiority.

Thought Process

Rhapsodics have a fast nervous system, causing shallowness and superficiality in their actions and decisions. It is frequent for them to come up with irrational fears and judgements. Having a fast nervous system may cause skipping over important details without giving them much thought. However, rhapsodics do not like skipping over any details, as they are extremely cautious. Thus, they get stuck on little details and are unable to come to a decision. Accompanied by having a weak nervous system, rhapsodics get overly stressed and anxious, ready to collapse. They do not cope well with stress and are prepared to give up.

There were times when I taught "*Mathematical Analysis*" for undergraduate students at King's College London. I had a student who was a member of rhapsodic psychotype. When I started teaching her "integration by parts", she started getting overly stressed. After only 15 minutes, she gave up and admitted that nothing would help her understand this concept. I calmed her down, and after 30 minutes, she started employing that technique perfectly, and we moved on to the next concept.

Why did she give up, though? How does the thought process of rhapsodics work exactly? Firstly, rhapsodics do not approach new things with enthusiasm as it means new responsibilities and the need to learn and get used to something new. As you can imagine, this is not ideal for rhapsodics as it will cause stress.

Secondly, they fear failures, and new concepts usually take time to grasp. I do not expect you to practice psychotype analysis in a perfect manner after reading this book once. It will take time for concepts to sink in, given you revise and reflect.

However, this situation is not ideal for rhapsodics. The longer it takes for rhapsodics to get used to something new, the more probable it is for them to think that they will fail. As they fear failure, it will cause them to get stressed and give up. In periods of extreme anxiety and mental exhaustion, hysterical explosions can be frequently observed in rhapsodics. But if you immediately get strict with them at this moment, then they will instantly calm down and listen to you attentively. This is because rhapsodics need strong people to confide confidence in them.

For example, assume your rhapsodic friend gives up on an important task and starts loudly complaining that the task is very difficult, he won't be able to do it and that there is not enough time, and thousand other reasons along with it. If, at this moment, you interrupt him in the middle of his speech with a firm and self-confident voice tone and posture, saying something like: *"Enough of your pessimism, we will indeed manage to overcome this"*, then he will mentally calm down. Rhapsodics simply need a firm assurance when they get mentally depleted. But be careful not to offend them. In no instance can you be disrespectfully loud or use insulting words or gestures. Be firm, rigid, and self-confident, but do not be dismantling.

Sometimes rhapsodics make commitments without understanding the responsibilities that come with it. This is due to two reasons. First, they fear saying "no" to people, as they fear it would hurt their relationship. This is due to their weak nervous system.

Second, when they are asked to do something, they do not realize the extent of things they would need to do as they approach it superficially. This is due to their fast nervous system. A fast and weak nervous system also affects the multitasking skills of rhapsodics. Each responsibility and line of work gives rhapsodics enough amount of stress, and therefore, taking on multiple tasks and responsibilities can be exhaustive.

That is why rhapsodics plan their work properly in advance and prioritize their responsibilities over anything in their social life. This can cause them to lose their friendships and connections when they start working. When their plans are disturbed, they get frustrated and worried.

I mentioned it already that rhapsodics have a low degree of self-esteem and tend to strong romantic partners as they want the support and approval of strong people when making decisions. For the same reason, rhapsodics easily get commanded over by others. And they find a certain degree of comfort in it. It does not only need to be someone commanding them what to do. The environment or system is enough.

For instance, rhapsodics enjoy a workplace with a strict set of rules and regulations or a profession with regular guidelines and responsibilities. These reduce uncertainty, indecisiveness, and the need for independent thinking. Though rhapsodics are intellectually curious and enjoy creative thinking, they prefer their responsibilities to be within systematic formats so that they are not exposed to making several independent decisions. Do not forget; rhapsodics are indecisive, lack resilience, and are risk-averse. When these three features are combined, then the need to make several independent decisions causes fear and anxiety.

For example, rhapsodic students usually become something we call a "teacher's pet". They do what their teachers tell them word to word as it is far easier to assume that your teacher is right rather than thinking that they might be wrong. Once you assume that they are right and that you need to do what they say, then there is nothing left for you to decide. Someone else has already decided for you what you need to do, and since you trust they are right, you go ahead and do it with a strong sense of comfort and pleasure. Otherwise, you will have to devise your own plan, do your own research and go through a significant degree of mental discomfort.

But no! Instead, you blindly assume that your teacher is right, as he is supposed to be. Teachers teach for a reason – they know better. Well, this is a very dangerous thought process. This is known as "***wishful thinking***", which defines such a thought process that tends to confide in comforting and pleasing beliefs rather than approaching things sceptically, rationally, or based on hard evidence. Rhapsodics are frequent victims of this. They build mental castles in their brain intended to prevent unwelcome ideas that may be rational or true, though contradictory to their own beliefs, values, and ideals. As such, they stubbornly contradict any thought that might discredit the person or belief that they have put their faith in.

I will give a personal example. I had a friend who studied with me during my undergraduate degree. He was a member of the rhapsodic psychotype who was taught that the higher are your grades, the easier it will be to become successful in life. You have to do your best in the class, and then opportunities will come down your way. All he did was study, and he got extremely competitive in it. I told him multiple times that grades were not enough, but he ignored me. Because it was far easier at that moment for him to continue doing what he was used to doing – to study.

He never listened to me when I asked him to attend corporate events, employer presentations, networking events, or extracurricular activities. He thought getting higher grades was far more important. After we graduated, he got to realize the hard truth. No opportunities came knocking to him, even though he was top of the class. He did not get any job offers from the companies he applied to, as he lacked experience since he did not engage in extracurricular activities or internships. He was not headhunted for opportunities, as he did not have a professional network. He understood that what he knew was wrong – putting blind trust in studying led him to despair.

Wishful thinking is dangerous, and we all fall victims to it without even knowing it. But rhapsodics tend to suffer severer consequences as it is harder for them to leave an idea or belief that they were holding on to. This would cause emptiness and uncertainty in their lives.

Did you know that when making bets, people become more optimistic about their choice the moment after making that bet? That is to say; if you buy a certain stock, say, Tesla, then you will start being far more optimistic about Tesla's price going up the moment after you made that bet, even though no new information presented is in favor of Tesla. This is because once you buy that stock, you have put your money at risk, and you know it. Thinking that price could go down and you could lose your money causes stress. But thinking that price would go up and you could win money causes comfort. Your brain immediately goes for the comforting thoughts – it wants to think about the scenario where you will win. Also, your mind does not want to exhaust itself by thinking about possible downsides or risks, as in these instances, you will need to think hard and long about what you should do? How should you cover your losses, and what other stocks should you then invest in or maybe not invest at all? How will you recover the money if you lose?

Here you lose your rationality – you start considering and analyzing scenarios that are biased towards stock price going up. If someone tells you that stock price could go down, e.g., let's say due to inflation concerns, then you are more likely to say, "*even if it happens, it is likely to be a short-term plump, and stock will recover sooner than you know*" compared to the moment when you have not made that purchase yet.

That is, you are more likely to come up with a "rational" reason for why the stock is a good buy after you have purchased it yourself. Simply, you will convince yourself that you have made the right choice. But you act so not because it is the rational thing to do but because it is comforting. This is the tragedy of wishful

271

thinking. This is one of the reasons why many investors and traders lose their money – they let comforting thoughts take over the uncomfortable yet rational thoughts.

Note: there is another reason why you are more likely to believe that the stock price is going to go up after buying that company's shares yourself. Everyone wants to align their thoughts with their actions. Once you purchase a stock, you start becoming more supportive of that company – an action of self-justification. You want to comfort yourself that you made the right decision, and the best way to do so is to devise reasons why that company is a good investment. This is a social influence tool known as "*consistency to commitments*", which implies that once you take a certain action, then your thought process becomes more supportive of that action. You can read more about it in Robert Cialdini's book, titled "Influence".

Overall, wishful thinking provides us with an easy way out when life's complex problems surround us. It is easy, fast, and effortless. It requires neither mental nor physical effort. As such, we live our lives comfortably and do not concern ourselves with many issues. For instance, many people think that climate change is not threatening simply because they assume government officials will not allow such a tragedy to come to pass, i.e., "*if any action is needed, they will certainly take it*". Well, good luck with that!

Social Relationships and External Appearance

Rhapsodics seek a comfort zone, just like epileptoids. After finding comfort in a certain group of friends, rhapsodics become less interested in making new acquaintances. If a hyperthymic will receive a unique enjoyment from meeting as many people as possible, rhapsodics enjoy having few but good friends. These are the people with whom he shares his life– his secrets, achievements, and troubles. The inner life of rhapsodics is hidden for outsiders, as these people are cautious and wary. They are not the initiators of conversations or relationships, and they can act in a somewhat awkward manner when someone approaches them to have a conversation.

Rhapsodics possess inertia as epileptoids. Once reaching a comfort zone, they do not want to change. They do not have strong adaptive skills and suffer from rapid shifts in their environments. Among all psychotypes, rhapsodics are the least likely to travel internationally for studying purposes. They get used to a family environment and are troubled about new lifestyle ideas. They may challenge themselves and overcome this trait, but many hardly do so.

Also, rhapsodics have a strong devotion and unconditional love towards their family. They try to deliver their parents' expectations as much as possible, but this puts extra pressure on them and can become exhausting (since rhapsodics get overwhelmed by responsibilities assigned to them).

Rhapsodics enjoy the company of smart people where intellectual debates, clever jokes, interesting events, and important news are shared and discussed. Rhapsodics have a strong degree of intellectual curiosity. They are interested in arts, music, and science. Similar to emotives, they love spending time with the natural environment, such as gardening, fishing, looking after animals or walking in a forest. These tend to destress them and reduce their anxiety.

Rhapsodics are also creative. Maybe not as creative as eccentric schizoids but still, they have something unique to offer. However, sometimes their ideas and opinions can be too out of context or even weird, causing surprise and irritation in people surrounding them.

Rhapsodics

Rhapsodics have a fast-paced and messy speech. They skip over many details, move from one argument to another, and therefore, cannot form solid arguments. Also, they do not like being talkative. Instead, they prefer listening to others.

Rhapsodics are not talkative because they are afraid of getting judged for their ideas or words. They do not want to take that risk, and hence, they play a passive role in social interactions. Furthermore, they can hardly initiate social interactions. For example, it is natural for a hyperthymic to meet and talk with new people without any hard effort. However, rhapsodics, just like schizoids, feel awkward and refrain from doing so. As such, they hardly approach people they do not know.

Rhapsodics possess a recessive character. Hence, they prefer to be in relationships with serious, strong, and dominant characters. They have a very compromising nature. Thus, their partners become very demanding and lead them wherever they want.

It becomes even worse if a rhapsodic is married to a fanatic – I can guarantee that the rhapsodic will never get the chance to speak his mind. Even worse, a fanatic partner will dominate the rhapsodic's personal life intensively, i.e., rhapsodic might end up not being allowed to meet his friends who are not married and cannot visit his family members whenever he wants, and so on. It is also not uncommon to see rhapsodics prefer partners who are far older than them. Emmanuel Macron, for example, is a member of rhapsodic psychotype:

Having said this, let's gradually discuss how rhapsodics look. Firstly, there are signs of stress on their face. You can see them biting their lips, clenching their teeth, licking their lips, crunching their fingers, rubbing their hands, blinking fast, and a natural grin. Rhapsodics tend to grin a lot, which is mostly developed as a natural adaptation to stress.

When they are stressed, rhapsodics widen their eyes and grin at the same time. We can observe this mimicry in the members of rhapsodic psychotype quite often, as they frequently get stressed. For example, if you look at the lips and cheeks of a rhapsodic, you will see that he is grinning. But if you look at his eyes and how tense his body is, you will see that he's under stress or fear. In primary schools, rhapsodic children often get shouted at as their teachers ask them, *"what are you smiling at"*. Well, they are smiling because they are under stress, and their teachers simply worsen the situation by badgering them further.

Rhapsodics tend to open their mouth when they are afraid while keeping their eyes wide. Such a facial expression under fear is indigenous to rhapsodics. I assume some of you have watched "*The Mummy*", a 1999 film. The character "*Beni Gabor*" portrayed by Kevin J. O'Connor, is a rhapsodic:

Although this movie character does not portray the best human being, he is still a member of the rhapsodic psychotype. I suggest you watch over some short YouTube videos to analyze his appearance, voice tone, and behavior.

It is very common for rhapsodics to be taken for granted, regardless of the quality and quantity of things that they do. When they overperform at their workplace, they hardly receive gratitude or praise. But if they ever fail once, then it will be immediately noticed and escalated.

Do you remember which psychotype was inclined to approach his colleagues with a lack of gratitude? Yes, the answer is the epileptoid psychotype. When rhapsodics work under the command of epileptoids, then they get exhausted and mentally depleted very often. It is also possible to observe periods of mental collapse or loss of self-control.

But why rhapsodics are being taken for granted more than the members of any other psychotype? Well, the answer is that these people rarely stand up for themselves and fight for their rights. This gives an impression of a weak and insecure individual. When people observe this, they get more comfortable in blaming or treating them unfairly.

Rhapsodics

To have a clear idea about rhapsodics, I would like to give an example from one film. Perhaps, all of you have watched "Harry Potter". The film's famous tripartite played the characters that animated different psychotypes: Potter – schizoid, Granger – hypothymic, McGonagall – epileptoid, and Weasley – rhapsodic.

Yes. Ronald Weasley was a typical rhapsodic. You can see how insecure, scared, worried, anxious, stressed and extremely risk-averse he was throughout the several scenes of the movies. For instance, when he first met Harry on the train, he was very shy and awkward in asking to let him in the cabin. Or recall his facial expressions when he encountered the spiders. I thought the poor boy will get a seizure from all that fear.

See some of his photos below:

Body Structures and Somatotypes

From the beginning of this book, I wanted to introduce you to reading people with their body structure, and I find that this part is the most suitable. Since you have already learned a lot of personality traits and covered almost all psychotypes, it will be far easier for you to grasp this point.

But let's begin with this; rhapsodics can be divided into two clusters, i.e., clusters of passives and aggressives. Passive rhapsodics have an asthenic body type, meaning feeble, long-limbed, narrow-shouldered, and narrow-chested, and weak muscular development. Aggressive rhapsodics, however, are like epileptoids. They are wide-shouldered, wide-chested, and possess good muscular development. Such muscular development occurs because these people keep their bodies tense due to stress.

Now, having studied types of rhapsodics, let's study somatotypes. But before studying this concept, I urge you not to rely on reading someone's personality through their body structure. The body structure of people may be informative of some personality traits of an individual or maybe informative of no personality traits.

According to American psychologist W. Sheldon, the body structure of people can be narrowly classified into three classes: endomorph (fat and round), mesomorph (muscular and athletic), and ectomorph (slim and straight). In the photo below, we have these three body structures in the respective order:

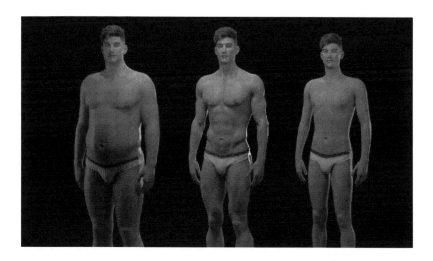

Endomorphs: The body type characterized by the first photo from the left hand side. Endomorphs tend to have a high degree of body muscle and fat. However, when endomorphs work out, they look more muscular than mesomorphs.

Mesomorphs: The body type characterized by the middle photo above. These people have a healthy weight. They have a muscular and athletic body type.

Ectomorphs: The body type characterized by the last photo above. Neither muscular nor fat. Narrow-chested and long-limbed. They struggle with gaining weight.

People usually have a combination of the two body types. For example, the best weightlifters are most usually endomorphic mesomorphs. Tennis players, on the other hand, are often ectomorphic mesomorphs. Long-distance runners are usually mesomorphic ectomorphs.

Now, Sheldon argued that:

- Endomorphs tend to be friendly, social, chill, and relaxed, but also lazy, selfish, and egoistic.

- Mesomorphs tend to be friendly, social, and extroverted, but also resilient, tough and competitive.

- Ectomorphs tend to be intelligent and calm but also introverted.

Although there is some truth in Sheldon's classification, there are also several inaccuracies and mistakes, and I personally dismiss the usefulness of his ideas as much as I dismiss the usefulness of the theory of "*Four Temperaments*" in reading people.

But there is a truth in the fact that certain psychotypes are likely to have a specific body type. In the table below, I have listed the names of psychotypes under each somatotype:

Character Trait	Most likely body structure	Least likely body structure
Histrionics	Mesomorphic	Ectomorphic
Epileptoids	Endomorphic or Mesomorphic	Ectomorphic
Hyperthymics	Somewhat Mesomorphic	None
Conformals	Ectomorphic	Mesomorphic
Schizoids	Ectomorphic	Mesomorphic
Narcissistics and Fanatics	Mesomorphic	Ectomorphic
Emotives	Somewhat Ectomorphic	Mesomorphic
Rhapsodics	None	None
Hypothymics	Ectomorphic or Endomorphic	Mesomorphic

Now, what shall you deduce from the table above? I have briefly stated the main ideas below:

- Histrionics are likely to have a mesomorphic body structure because they enjoy working out and having a good body structure. They love taking their good-looking half-naked photos and posting them on social media platforms. They are least likely to become endomorphic as they take care of their external appearance seriously.

- Epileptoids generally have a muscular body structure, so they are likely to have mesomorphic body structure at young ages, but when they start working, they begin developing inertia. At this point, to deal with stress, they often start drinking and eating more than the recommended amount. As such, they start gaining weight, and their body starts looking more and more endomorphic. But even when they are overweight, they have a wide chest and muscular shoulders.

- Hyperthymics are social and active and enjoy sports. So, it is likely for them to develop a mesomorphic body type. Hyperthymics have somewhat muscular arms and shoulders. Their chest is not narrow, but it is hardly wide. As such, they are somewhat mesomorphic. But this may change as they age and start being less and less active. With a poor diet, they may either gain weight and look more like an endomorph, or lose muscle mass, and look more like an ectomorph.

- Conformals mostly have an ectomorphic body type, meaning linear and narrow. They are not inclined towards sports.

- Schizoids do not care much about their external appearance. They are very calm and do not have the desire to look good to others. As such, they are least likely to be mesomorphic. There can be only two explanations for a schizoid to be mesomorphic: he either developed self-consciousness on his external appearance and agreed that it is important to look good, or he sees bodybuilding as a hobby. Do not forget; schizoids follow their passions. So, if they are passionate about sports, it is likely for them to build an athletic body. Nonetheless, most schizoids do not fall into these categories. Hence, they do not develop from an ectomorph into a mesomorph. But they can become endomorphic through unhealthy lifestyles, e.g., they can start gaining weight. However, you will still see the signs of ectomorphic body structure, even if they are overweight. You have to pay attention to their chest. Gaining weight does not widen your chest, so they are likely to become overweight but with a narrow chest.

- Narcissistics and fanatics enjoy sports as it is a healthy life habit. Hence, they tend to have a somewhat mesomorphic body type. However, some narcissistics and fanatics may be so focused on their work that they may not make time for exercise and eventually start gaining body mass.

- Emotives are gentle and calm and enjoy harmony. Lifting heavy weights or undergoing strenuous physical activities are not their natural forte. Hence, they are not likely to have a mesomorphic body structure. Most likely, they will have a somewhat ectomorphic body type, but their chests won't be as narrow as in schizoids.

- Rhapsodics do not have a "most likely" or "least likely" body structure. All three body structures may be equally observed in the members of this psychotype. For instance, rhapsodics may decide to overcome their stress through strenuous physical activity, which would eventually make them mesomorphic, or through eating and drinking a lot, making them endomorphic. Aggressive rhapsodics are equally likely to be either endomorphic or mesomorphic, while passive rhapsodics are most likely to be ectomorphic.

- Hypothymics are not taught yet, but you can revisit this part after reading them. Hypothymics do not excel in sports or physical activities; hence, they are not likely to build a muscle mass. They can also eat or drink in an unhealthy way, leading them to become endomorphic.

Pathological Accentuation of Rhapsodics and Dependent Personality Disorder

The pathological accentuation of rhapsodic psychotype is similar to people with **Dependent Personality Disorder (DPD)**, combined with some *obsessive-compulsive features*. Since we already covered OCPD, let's begin with the Dependent Personality Disorder. Later, I will briefly go over the OCPD personality traits that are often observed in rhapsodics as well. I will also mention the OCPD traits that are not observed in rhapsodics.

So, DPD characterizes people with a psychological dependence on others for their psychological and physical needs. Also, people with this disorder often have strong feelings of fear and anxiety, just like rhapsodics. These feelings are stronger towards people whom they rely on the most. They especially fear and get anxious about thoughts of losing these people or not being equally loved and appreciated by them.

Both rhapsodics and people with DPD hardly heal from breakups. When their relationships with people to whom they were close to come to an end, the feelings of devastation, depression, anxiety, and immense stress take over their daily responsibilities.

In such moments, these people start underperforming or not performing at all. **Pathological Demand Avoidance (PDA)**, which describes a condition when an individual disregards and ignores his demands at a considerable level, is a frequent trait to observe in people suffering from DPD.

Rhapsodics do not suffer from PDA unless they have gone through a breakup. Although rhapsodics and people with DPD feel devastated and suffer from PDA when their close relationships end, it only lasts for a short time until they form a close relationship with someone new. What is commonly observed in rhapsodics and people with DPD is that they seek new relationships and companionships when their relationships with people they were very close to come to an end.

People with DPD face difficulties in making regular daily decisions without seeking advice and help. Gladly, in the lack of excessive accentuation, rhapsodics are not so incapable of making daily decisions. Although they will be hesitant or double-check their decisions, they will still take ownership of their tasks.

I previously mentioned that rhapsodics hardly disagree with others as they fear damaging their relationship. Also, they lack self-confidence in criticising someone because usually, a rhapsodic will trust others' judgements over his. And it is for the lack of self-confidence that rhapsodics hardly take initiatives.

Before concluding this part, let's discuss which traits of OCPD pathologically accentuated rhapsodics have and which ones they do not. Rhapsodics and pathological rhapsodics have the following traits that are in common with OCPD:

- The overwhelming need for punctuality
- Strong obedience to rules and regulations
- Devotion to work
- Frugality with money

Rhapsodics and pathological rhapsodics **do not** have the following traits of OCPD:

- Stiff, tough, and rigid manners
- Strong sense of righteousness
- Strong ownership and desire for complete control over the individual task

Let's end this section with Pinkofsky's mnemonic for the dependent personality disorder. He has used the term "R E L I A N C E" for these people:

R	Reassurance needed when making decisions
E	Expressing disagreements is difficult due to fear of loss of support or approval
L	Life responsibilities often assumed and set by others
I	Initiation is difficult due to lack of self-confidence
A	Alone (feels helpless and uncomfortable when alone)
N	Nurturance (goes to excessive lengths to obtain nurturance and support)
C	Companionship (another relationship) sought urgently when a close relationship ends
E	Exaggerated fears of being left to care for self

Conclusion

Rhapsodics are risk-averse, cautious, anxious, and stressed people. The lack of resilience and a strong sensitivity towards negative events arise from the weakness of the nervous system. Because these people fear uncertainty, they want to account for all the details. This requires a somewhat gradual nervous system. But since the members of this psychotype have a fast nervous system, they go over the same details quickly over and over again, without coming to a decision. And the more time it takes for them to conclude, the more and more frustrated and anxious they become.

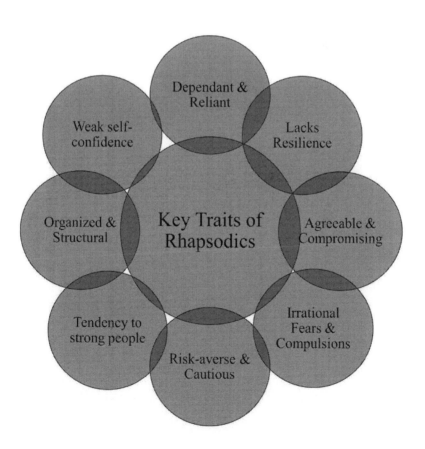

10

Hypothymics

If one stole all my sorrow, he would be to me a thief,
Since inexistence of sorrow would become my grief

(Bakhtiyar Vahabzada, Azerbaijani Poet)

The members of this psychotype are people who prefer a passive life. Hypothymic consists of words: "hypo" and "thymic", meaning "low-spirited". These are people who naturally have a weak and low degree of energy, mood, and enthusiasm. Pessimism is among the key traits of hypothymics as they tend to focus mainly on potential risks and errors rather than on benefits and rewards. But if you would describe these people as pessimists, they would disagree. They like to envision themselves as "realists". They believe it is important to hedge the risks and focus on all the possible negatives in order to guarantee a positive result. However, even if they achieve a positive result, they do not take the time to appreciate it.

Hypothymics and people with depression have some traits in common. In fact, hypothymics are characterized as "depressives" by some profilers. But I do not like such characterization of hypothymics as there many differences between these people. Table below summarizes their similarities and differences:

Features of Hypothymics also observed in Depression	Features of Hypothymics not observed in Depression	Features of Depression not observed in Hypothymics
Pessimism and Moroseness	Perfectionism and Orderliness	Insomnia or Hypersomnia
Low degree of energy, mood and activitiy	Hardworking and Efficient	Poor eating or drinking habits
Low degree of self-confidence and self-esteem	Accurate and Punctual	Poor concentration
Escaping loud and crowded environments	Organised, Systematic and Structural	Avoiding responsibilities
Introversion and Passivity	Attentive to detail	Feeling hopeless
Anhedonia	Informative and Thorough	Inflicting blame and punishment on oneself
Reduced Affect Display	Quality-oriented	Sensitivity towards criticisms
Lack of excitement, motivation and satisfaction, even from the greatest of achievements	Logical and Rational	Seeking care and attention
Ignoring positive occurences	Cautious and Risk-averse	Inflicting blame and punishment on oneself
Tendency towards exaggerating negative issues	Critical thinking (though inclined towards exagerrating the negative)	Frequent feelings of sadness when alone

There are two traits above that I have not taught yet: **Reduced Affect Display** and **Anhedonia**. I will start this chapter with these traits as they are particularly interesting but also very important.

Anhedonia and Flat Affect

I have previously taught you hedonism when studying histrionics. The opposite of hedonism is known as anhedonia, which is commonly characterized as the *inability* to experience or enjoy pleasure, and reduced motivation. Although anhedonia is a core symptom in people with depressive disorders, the members of the hypothymic psychotype *somewhat resemble* this trait as well.

By highlighting "*somewhat resemble,*" I am trying to emphasize that hypothymics have the ability to experience pleasure; that is to say, they do not have any mental or behavioral disorder inhibiting them from enjoying things. Anhedonia is referred to as the inability to experience pleasure, and if you say that hypothymics have anhedonia, you'd be mistaken. Hypothymics resemble anhedonia, but they do not have it. For instance, hypothymics do not enjoy talking positively about themselves, even if they achieve something great. But it does not mean they do not feel great about it – they simply do not show it.

Anhedonia is a common symptom observed in disorders such as **Dysthymia** (also known as **Persistent Hypothymic Mood**), **Schizophrenia, Bipolar Disorder,** and so on. As said previously, hypothymics do not have anhedonia. They rather have a lower tendency to seek and enjoy pleasure compared to the members of other psychotypes. Let's give another example. One symptom of anhedonia is escaping social gatherings, friendly environments, and crowded publics. Hypothymics naturally possess this trait as well since they tend towards social solitude.

Although hypothymics seek the care and love of their friends and miss them frequently when alone, they tend to get bored with them relatively quickly. This is because hypothymics have a low capacity for social interactions. As hypothymics get overwhelmed from people very quickly, they tend to return to their comfort zone. The comfort zone of hypothymics is isolated from the outside world, e.g., their room or flat. They hardly get out for some fun or physical activity and spend most of their time in their comfort zone, where they are isolated from the outside world.

One of the main symptoms of people with anhedonia is the ***Reduced Affect Display (RAD)***. This is a condition where one exhibits a low degree of emotional reactivity. In other words, it is characterized as the inability to express feelings and emotions, such as care, love, worry, or compassion. I have a very close friend who possesses this condition. We were used to living together for a while, and whenever I told him about something unpleasant happening in my life, he seemed to be extremely indifferent. This is because people with RAD hardly express their emotions verbally or nonverbally. And for this reason, others think that these people do not care when you share your sorrow or problems with them.

Reduced affect display has three degrees in relation to its severity: ***constricted affect***, ***blunted affect*** and ***flat affect***. Constricted affect is the least severe as it describes the condition where the individual has a lower degree of emotional expressions compared to the average person. He still expresses emotions here and there, but we cannot say that he does so frequently.

Blunted affect is more severe than constricted affect but less severe than flat affect. This is the condition where the individual may express some forms of emotions, but extremely rarely and with a significantly reduced intensity. Blunted affect is frequently observed in people who experience some form of physical or psychological bullying, especially from their parents. When a child is bullied, he starts to learn to hide his emotions. Such a child (wrongly) assumes that by hiding his emotions, he will hide his weaknesses. This behavior becomes a permanent personality and resembles itself at all stages of adulthood.

Flat affect is the most severe form of RAD. People with flat affect have no or almost no emotional expressions. This is one of the most common traits observed in psychopathy. For this reason, it is not a trait to be studied in this book.

Hypothymics have a constricted affect, i.e., they do express their emotions, but they do so infrequently. People with a constricted affect have a calm voice tone. Their facial expressions do not change rapidly – a trait that clearly distinguishes these people from histrionics. I believe the main reason for these people to have a constricted affect is that they approach everything logically and rationally instead of emotionally. If something bad happens, these people prefer to think about it in an analytical way to find a solution instead of getting emotional over it. Therefore, hypothymics rarely get angry, anxious or frustrated. As such, hypothymics are resilient and work well under crisis.

There is an important nuance that should be carefully accounted for. Although people with anhedonia often have RDA, having or resembling RDA does not necessarily mean having anhedonia. RDA refers to the inability to show emotions, not to lack of emotions or not having emotions. Anhedonia, on the other hand, refers to the inability to enjoy emotions, such as pleasure. That is why we use the word "display" in RAD – it is a display.

Thought Process

Hypothymics are the ones who keep everything in order. They have a systematic and structural approach to everything. The degree of their orderliness and tidiness dwarf even that of epileptoids. When it comes to punctuality, hypothymics are the best at it. These people arrange their plans, meetings and commitments meticulously.

People employ various forms of thought when working towards a goal. Hyperthymics, for instance, focus only on the benefits of achieving a certain goal. They tend to exaggerate the gains and ignore the associated risks. Hypothymics, on the other hand, focus on risks and think of the ways to hedge them. They do not motivate themselves from positive results. That is to say; they do not motivate themselves by envisioning the benefits of achieving a certain goal.

Because hypothymics do not feel motivated through positive results, motivating them with pure words is pretty much impossible. These people are the least to be affected by a pep talk. What do you think is the reason behind this?

Well, pep talks are brief and emotional in nature. By being brief, it lacks details. Indeed, hypothymics find pep talks stupid, foolish and ineffective. I know hypothymics who treat people who get affected by pep talks as dumb. Since pep talks target the emotionality of people rather than rationality, it does not work with hypothymics. If you want to influence them, remove all emotionality and talk purely from the rational viewpoint. A detailed, accurate, comprehensive and logical flow of argument will influence them easily.

Because hypothymics are accurate, responsible, logical and quality-oriented, they are most suitable for technical fields. For example, programming, engineering, financial modelling and so on. I know a hypothymic who is a director at Goldman Sachs. He told me that he enjoyed his time as an analyst more than his time as a director, even though his current earnings are considerably higher than before. This is because analysts work on financial modelling, research and computations, while directors meet with clients, conduct team meetings and so on. As such, hypothymics are well suited to positions requiring strong technical knowledge yet minimal interaction with people.

Hypothymics get caught up in details when working towards something. Working with these people on tight deadlines can be extremely challenging. Why? Well, because these people try to build a comprehensive solution. They are perfectionists in nature. They want to account for every single detail before finalising the task. And this is the main difference between hypothymics and epileptoids. Although epileptoids tend to account for details as well, they are extremely pragmatic and reach solutions rather quickly.

In contrast, hypothymics check every single detail twice or thrice. And even this is not enough for them to finalise the project. They proceed with putting all the pieces together and looking at the overall model. Afterward, they change things here and there. Then they look at the overall model again. And then again, they change things here and there. They continue doing so repeatedly. They aim to perfect the model. As you might remember, perfectionism is not a trait possessed by epileptoids.

Research is the forte of hypothymics. They would easily sit behind their desks and research every piece of information that is relevant to a particular problem. For them, there is not anything like "too much information". Every piece of information is important. Once they feel they have got a somewhat *sufficient* degree of information, they analyze all of it to develop a solution. But this process can be time-consuming. Hypothymics have their own pace of thought and work. And they like to progress at a slow pace to account for everything. They do not like to get rushed.

So, keep this in mind when working with these people. If you need hypothymics to complete the work by Friday, then set the deadline for Wednesday. They'll indeed not deliver it by Wednesday. But if they do not feel rushed or criticised for failing the deadline, they will assume that they can take a longer time to complete the task. So, ensure to chase them on Tuesday, remind them of tomorrow's deadline and ask for an update. When they inform you that they'll fail the deadline, express your disappointment and ask them to complete it as soon as possible. Set the deadline within the next 24 hours. This way, you can ensure you'll get your project in time.

Hypothymics are not solution-oriented. They enjoy the process more than the solution itself. Some might suggest they are not target-driven. And they actually would be right. They enjoy the trip more than the destination. When working towards something, hypothymics take a cautious approach of analysing and perfecting everything. They enjoy performing all the technical work in an accurate and cautious manner. They love to get to the bottom of things. And often, they do not finish anything – there is always more to do.

Epileptoids, once finishing a certain task, never remember of it again. It needed to be done and it is done. And they try finishing tasks as quickly as possible. They just want to get it out of hand. They want to reduce the number of things they are overwhelmed with. But hypothymics are not as such. Because they hardly finalize anything, they find themselves involved in multiple outstanding tasks. As time goes by, these people start to suffer from a lot of background stress.

Background stress usually occurs when the number of things that we neglect starts to accumulate. It usually coincides with the busy periods at work or university. Procrastination is the main contributor to background stress. But hypothymics accumulate the background stress not only from procrastination but also from not finalizing their tasks. They just keep doing what can be finished. They extend the duration of the process. But life cannot be devoted to working only one thing. There are a lot of things progressing in our lives, such as at school or work. As the new things that require attention start to accumulate, the older things that are yet to be finished start causing background stress.

Hypothymics suffer from procrastination as well. This is one of the main differences between them and epileptoids. If an epileptoid finishes an outstanding task as quickly as possible in order to get it out of hand (without compromising the quality, though), a hypothymic will not start until he feels ready. He needs to access everything before starting something. He also needs to access whether he would have the time. More often than not, they do not have the time since there are many outstanding tasks yet to be finished. As such, they find themselves in positions where they cannot move forward. Such instances of stagnation, in turn, can lead to prolonged periods of lethargy and apathy. The lack of motivation, as a result, leads to procrastination. On such occasions, the motivation of hypothymics for embarking on something new or finishing an existing task completely diminishes. Hence, they find themselves in a stagnant position.

Hypothymics love following instructions. This is a trait that they share with psychasthenics. They enjoy performing tasks with clear guidelines. They are procedural in nature. They almost memorize the instructions before starting to work on a task. And they frequently revisit those instructions throughout the process. This way, they ensure that everything appears the way it should. Quality shall never be compromised.

I would like to ask you a question. Do you think hypothymics have motivation and skills to reach their targets, or even a bigger question, do these people have targets? The answer is yes, they do, and they achieve them successfully. Hypothymics are disciplined, systematic and structural, organized and hardworking. They set targets for themselves and do their best to achieve them. But they do not get excited by it once they achieve it: *"there is always more that could have been done"*.

Hypothymics are not good in motivation. When they try motivating their staff in achieving a certain target, instead of explaining the positive things that would be achieved, they focus on the things that would be lost in case of a failure. For example, if a hypothymic is heading a climate-support project and assuming that his team is assembling a device that would reduce CO_2 emissions, he would try motivating his staff by saying something like: *"if we fail to build this on time, then we will be responsible for every damage caused to our planet from these emissions"*. But he could motivate his staff in a positive manner, by saying: *"we will manage, and we will serve a great deal in tackling the climate issue. We will leave the world in a better condition than we found it"*. Overall, hypothymics seek motivation by focusing on the negatives. As such, they are inclined towards preventing problems from happening rather than coming with creative initiatives.

Hypothymics do not welcome changes. Their adaptation skills are weak because they do not like abandoning their comfort zone. As with epileptoids, inertia and apathy are common personality traits observed in these people. They prefer following procedures and employing standard processes instead of adopting something new and taking the initiative. For this reason, hypothymics lack entrepreneurial skills. Furthermore, hypothymics lack creative thinking skills. Instead of thinking outside the box and coming up with a clever solution to a problem, hypothymics prefer searching for the tools within the box and employing them in a standard manner. Getting outside the scope is not a trait possessed by the members of this character.

I want to ask you a question. Imagine you are a member of a team led by hypothymic and that all of you have successfully delivered an important project on which you were working for a long period of time. Now, suppose that your boss announces that all of you will get a good bonus for. When hearing this news, how would you react? Well, after a short moment of excitement, someone in the team would definitely offer to go to get some drinks. And now, imagine all of you are collectively preparing to go to the bar. Who do you think would start quietly making his way out and leaving you all?

Of course, your hypothymic boss! Indeed, you will drag him with you in the end, but he will be reluctant and offer not to go, saying things like, "*you guys go and have fun*". One reason for this is that hypothymics do not feel included in a group. They feel like they do not belong or are not enjoyed by others, which is true, as no one enjoys the company of morose and pessimistic people for a long period of time. Everyone prefers the company of enthusiastic and positive people. If you want people to chase you, ensure that you are enthusiastic when speaking to them. Be positive and open-minded, do not criticise people, and do not argue on unnecessary topics. Have fun and ensure people around you enjoy themselves as well.

Because hypothymics possess critical thinking skills that are skewed towards negatives, most hypothymics tend to become critics. Assume you come up with an interesting idea that could make for an attractive business proposal, and you decide to share it with your friend, who is a member of the hypothymic psychotype. Suppose you tell him that you are going to start an electric car company. His first response would be: "*you do not have any experience in this area; you will fail*". Assume you counter by saying: "*I will create a team of successful engineers; I already found people suitable for this initiative*". How do you think a hypothymic will respond in this case?

Well, he will most certainly say: "*well, good luck in trusting them*". As you can see, regardless of what you say, they mainly focus on the negatives. Well, you might assume that he is being reasonable, but here is the thing. Instead of suggesting problems, he could advise and support his friend in ways to overcome those problems. Or give some advice on things that his friend could do to be more successful in this area. Nobody enjoys cynicism. You must ensure that you label rewards as much as you label risks, if not more. It is a far better idea to seek motivation from future rewards first, and once motivated, spend your time on overcoming problems that could arise in the future and maybe trying to prevent them in the first place.

Social Relationships and External Appearance

Hypothymics tend to be knowledgeable. Because they love research, they tend to have vast erudition. Combined with being systematic, talented and skilled, these people are capable of solving the most challenging problems. If they could be somewhat more solution-oriented, that is to say, driven to finish the tasks as soon as possible, then they would be the most competent people to work with.

However, hypothymics do not praise themselves as such. It is not like they value humility as a personality trait. Rather they do not see any point in praising themselves or craving the approval of others. They do not feel prideful when someone praises them. They put logic and rationality over emotionality. Why would a rational and logical person need the approval of others, right? What is the point behind it?

Assume you have a hypothymic colleague who saved you and the whole team from the burden of completing a back-breaking, challenging task. He completed it before any of you figured out the solution. You might all praise him for this and even offer to treat him with a drink. But his reply would probably be as such: *"it is no matter; I was just doing my job"*.

It is not like these people are not aware of their skills. Quite the opposite. They know exactly what they can do and what they cannot do. But they do not feel the need to toot their own horns. They just do what they do, and they do not need to be praised for it. But it does not mean that you can underappreciate them. Hypothymics would never allow anyone to speak lowly of their talents. Throw mud at them, and they will throw it back at you. And if you challenge them on a topic that they are knowledgeable about, then be prepared for a heated discussion. They would not let go of you until you prove them wrong or accept that you are wrong. But it is my advice that you do not attempt to prove them wrong. If anything, listen to them attentively as you might genuinely learn a thing or two.

So, if you are talking and there is a hypothymic around, do not make a mistake. If you say something that is not right, then a hypothymic will notice it immediately. Then he will start to talk about it. Embrace yourself for a pedantic, long and boring speech with dozens of details that are absolutely uninteresting, unnecessary and redundant for the sake of your argument. That is right. Even if the mistake that you made has absolutely no impact on the validity of your argument, a hypothymic will not care. You said something wrong, and it is his solemn duty to correct you.

Do not get me wrong. Their intention is not to prove you wrong or to get the attention of others. Simply, these people cannot help themselves if they see or hear a mistake. I think we have all met such people in classrooms. These are the ones who like to argue with the teachers or lecturers. They would raise their finger and make a statement by camouflaging it as a question. And that statement is pretty obvious: *"uh, excuse me, but that does not seem to be right"*. Also, these people like to answer all the questions. They cannot wait to demonstrate their knowledge.

Hypothymics

I would like you to visualise these people. Most often, they do not give a dime on the opinions of others. Their own opinion is all that matters for them. But to us, they appear as unbearable people who cannot live another second without demonstrating how knowledgeable they are. As such, they are usually the ones who are labelled as "know-it-all". But do not treat this behavior of hypothymics badly. They do not have any malicious intentions behind their behavior. If you accept these people the way they are, it will be easier for you to communicate with them.

I would like to give a fictional example for a hypothymic psychotype. The character "Hermione Granger" from the "Harry Potter" is a typical hypothymic:

How many friends do you think hypothymics have? You guessed right. Not many. Some hypothymics do not even have any friends. It is not like they do not want to, but they are very selective. When they befriend someone, it is for real. They will genuinely care for that person, and the relationship will probably last for a lifetime. But it is challenging for them to accept someone as their friend. Usually, hypothymics get along with schizoids or other hypothymics. Because schizoids are people with high intellectual capabilities, hypothymics highly admire them. Hypothymics enjoy talking to schizoids. Because both psychotypes are pedantic in nature, they do not get bored or irritated from the pedanticism of one another.

In addition to being selective in their friends, hypothymics are highly introverted people. Unlike hyperthymics or histrionics, they cannot tolerate noisy environments, at least for a long time. When going to parties or other social gatherings, these people are the ones to leave first. But interestingly, if they get drunk, they will feel the euphoric states of alcohol. And that is my advice to you. Get hypothymics drunk if you want to have a great time with them. They will overcome their social barriers very easily once in a drunken state. In fact, they become hyperthymic if they get to have one too many drinks.

Hypothymics

Do you think hypothymics are emotional? Not in a sense that "do they have emotions", as all people do, but rather in a sense if they express their emotions? Usually, hypothymics are not people to discuss or express emotions. It does not even cross their minds. The partners of hypothymics often complain about this, e.g., *"you never say how much you love me..."*. But this is the case with hypothymics. They do not realize that people need attention, praise, admiration, love and care. Because hypothymics are very independent, they expect everyone else to be the same, as it is the most "logical" thing to do. And they are right if you ask me. But people are emotional, so we have to treat them in a considerate manner.

Hypothymics are closed. If they do not know you well, you should keep your distance. Do not crack jokes with them if you have not known them for a long time. And do not ask them any personal questions. They will not like it, and they will not respond to you either. These people require a lot of personal space. So, do not put yourself in an awkward position. Furthermore, keep a certain distance from them. I mean literally – keep at least half a meter distance. If you get too close to them, they will step back or inform you to step back. Both situations would feel pretty embarrassing.

Hypothymics do not open up to people easily. They hardly talk to others about what is going on in their lives. They neither want nor need to discuss their personal issues with others. Even if they achieve something great, they will not share it with people. For instance, assume you have a hypothymic colleague who recently starred in a movie. Do you think he will share this information with you? Not likely. Unless you are his close friend, do not expect him to open up to you about anything.

Hypothymics have a low degree of energy, and they do not have an active social life. They hardly communicate with people who are not very close to them. The voice tone of hypothymics is low and slow, and they cannot think quickly on their feet. They are neither witty nor whimsical. Passivity in personal relationships with their partners leads to many conflicts. Hypothymics never facilitate or initiate any form of activity with their friends or partners.

Their friends, after some time, start distancing themselves as they do not want to be the only one in the relationship who suggests meeting up. Every person wants to be chased and feel valued once in a while. Partners of hypothymics complain about the lack of compassion and attention, which are the primary causes of conflict. In such instances, hypothymics freeze – they cannot come up with any reason or excuse and tend to either run from the problem by ignoring it or distancing themselves from their friends or partners. Or they surrender. In the latter case, they apologize and promise to change. However, they fail to deliver such promises as these people are not skilled in expressing emotions. This leads to further conflicts and disappointments.

Hypothymics have psychological barriers when seeking people out or engaging in activities that would develop the relationship. They are not good at giving or receiving gifts. Gestures, surprises, compliments, or other forms of expression of love, care, or appreciation are not for the members of this psychotype. It is not because they are not genuine in their emotions or do not have emotions; it is simply because they are not capable of expressing them (remember RDA). For this reason, it is not a good idea to build expectations on hypothymics that they will not deliver.

In fact, building expectations and opinions on people is not a good idea, neither positive nor negative. I assume most of you would understand why forming negative opinions on people is not good, but what about forming good opinions and expectations? The problem is that the more you think about a person positively, the more emotionally you are going to get attached to that person, while nothing material changes in your relationship – it is all in your head. You are forming expectations.

After some time, you will get disappointed since the person will fail to deliver your expectations. But because you have unintentionally developed an emotional attachment, it gets harder for you to distance yourself. It is our natural tendency to exaggerate the positive traits of people about whom we think frequently, and this is not a rational course of action. So, I strongly advise all of you not to, under any conditions, form positive expectations or opinions about anyone, or think too often about them, regardless of how close you think you are. Or how close you think you could get.

Conclusion

Well, we have concluded the last of the main psychotypes and congratulations on making it this far. I hope learning about hypothymics was enjoyable. Again, these people appear as "know-it-all", and many of you might have wrong biases against such people. Mostly, we think that these people act the way they do to get attention, show off, or belittle others. None of it is the case. If these people know something, they will free to say it. They will never say anything that they are not sure about. Keeping close company with such people is always useful. These people are very knowledgeable, have vast erudition and are very competent in their field of work. The only problem is that they prolong the process and extend the timeline. So, keep this in mind and track their progress carefully.

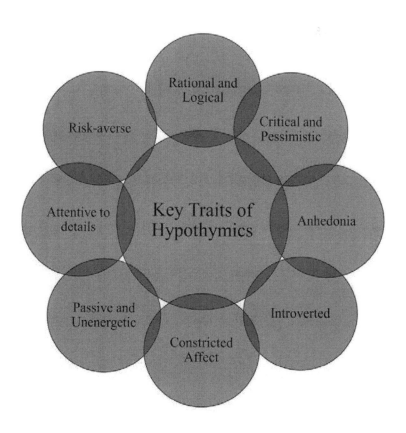

Epilogue

I find a profound pride to propose this book on personality psychology to you. I am hoping that it will help you identify people much better. Normal people judge others based on the way they look. The smarter people judge others based on what their actions mean. The smartest bunch judge others based on the reasons behind their actions. This book was just about understanding the reasons behind actions. This way, you will be able to predict the actions of people constantly and, combined with your wisdom, develop an influential and efficient means of communication.

My purpose in writing this book was to demonstrate the several forms of human character that remained a mystery up until now. Every individual has a unique personality that consists of their beliefs, attitudes, morals, values. But our character constitutes the significant chunk of our personality, if not the most of it. Our character dictates how we act and behave and think and speak. But despite its importance, there is not a single piece of work on this topic that has been proposed to the international community to read, study and judge. And that is why, I feel pride and glory in being the pioneer in this field.

Nonetheless, the mastery of psychotypes is one of the most important skills to acquire. Understanding various personalities and being able to work with them and even influence them is the most desired skill in any field. By mastering this field, you are mastering leadership. The topics covered in this book provide us with all the means we need to develop any form of a personal relationship with anyone, whether it is a friendship or romance. The way you treat people and how effectively you communicate will determine the course of your relationship with them.

Probably, you understood that effective communication is all about adjusting your speech, words, tone and attitude towards the listener. Different characters will react differently to what you say. Whatever it is that you try to delegate, it will be processed through the mental mechanisms of the listener. His character will have an important role in determining his response. Therefore, you should adjust yourself towards the characters of people you are communicating with. This way, you will be achieving results in a faster and more efficient manner.

One of the most common fallacies is to *"treat people the way you'd like to be treated"*. This is basically not true. The way we would like to be treated directly depends on our character. For this reason, we naturally tend to get along with people who share our psychotype. However, most people will have a psychotype that differs from ours. So, how do we manage the majority? Well, we cannot simply project our personality traits onto others. Therefore, we need to adjust our attitude when dealing with different people.

Take histrionics, for example. You already know that these people want to be treated with attention and care, while quite the opposite is true for hypothymics. The latter prefers keeping distance from people. So, if you are a hypothymic and if you treat a histrionic the way you'd like to be treated yourself, then you'll fail. If you want to formulate a good relationship with histrionics, then you have to praise, compliment and be attentive towards them. As such, as a hypothymic, you'll need to adjust your attitude by 180 degrees. And this might be challenging.

This concept of adjusting our attitude applies to all people. All you need to do is to study their personality traits carefully and treat them accordingly. In the beginning, it will not be easy to adjust yourself towards various forms of human character. But after some practice, you'll get it. Also, by practicing this, you will develop strong awareness. This is because a person who constantly pays attention to the personality traits of others, tries to identify their psychotype and determines how he should adjust his character to effectively communicate with them gradually becomes a person who is highly aware of himself and others.

But it is important to understand that such adjustments can only last for short periods. Simply put, you'll not be able to tolerate performing the actions and behaviors that are not compatible with your core psychotype for a prolonged period of time. As a schizoid or an analytic hypothymic, for example, you might be able to perform as a hyperthymic for a night when going out with a group of friends. But this will likely exhaust you the next day, and you'll need to take a day or two to "fix" your mental health. Although adjusting our character is the best thing to do when meeting others, it is important to understand that it will become counterproductive if this process lasts for too long.

I wish you found the information presented in this book useful and had a great time going through it. It is up to you how you will use the information presented here in your daily lives. I strongly believe that if you use the concepts taught in this book to a good degree, then it will definitely lead to success in any field that you want to move forward. I hope you enjoyed this book as much as I enjoyed writing it. And I hope you'll make the most out of it.

Bibliography

Carnegie, D. (2009). *"How to Win Friends and Influence People"*. New York: Simon & Schuster.

Cialdini, R. (1984). *"Influence. The Psychology of Persuasion"*. New York, NY: William Morrow e Company.

Ekman, P. (2007). *"Emotions Revealed: Recognizing Faces and Feelings to Improve Communication and Emotional Life"*. New York: Henry Holt.

Erikson, T. (2019). *"Surrounded by Idiots"*. St. Martins Essentials.

Gannushkin, P.B. (1933). *"Manifestations of psychopathies: statics, dynamics, systematic aspects"*.

Goleman, D. (2005). *"Emotional Intelligence: Why It Can Matter More Than IQ"*. New York: Bantam.

Greene, R., & Elffers, J. (2000). *"The 48 laws of power"*.

Hurlbert, D. F., & Apt, C. (1994). *"Female sexual desire, response, and behavior"*. Behavior Modification, 18(4), 488–504.

Lichko, A. E. (1982). *"Psychopathies and Accentuation of Character of Teenagers"*.

Sukhareva, G. (1959). *"Sukhareva GE, Clinical lectures on children's psychiatry"*.

Milgram, S., and J. Sabini. (1975). *"On Maintaining Norms: A Field Experiment in the Subway"*. Unpublished manuscript, City University of New York.

Millon, T., & Millon, T. (2004). *"Personality disorders in modern life"*. Hoboken, N.J: Wiley.

Printed in Great Britain
by Amazon